HUNTERS

Hunter FGA.9 XJ695/Q of 58 Squadron based at RAF Wittering, 1973. (*Richard Wilson*)

HUNTERS

THE HAWKER HUNTER IN BRITISH MILITARY SERVICE

Martin W. Bowman

SUTTON PUBLISHING

First published in the United Kingdom in 2002 by
Sutton Publishing Limited · Phoenix Mill
Thrupp · Stroud · Gloucestershire · GL5 2BU

British Library Cataloguing in Publication Data
A catalogue record for this book is available from the British Library

ISBN 0 7509 2935 9

FGA.9 XG237/T of 8 Squadron undergoing engine runs on its Avon 207 at Khormaksar following replacement of the power unit, October 1962. (*Ray Deacon*)

Typeset in 10/14 pt Sabon.
Typesetting and origination by
Sutton Publishing Limited.
Printed and bound in England by
J.H. Haynes & Co. Ltd, Sparkford.

Contents

Acknowledgements vii

Chapter 1 **Hunter's Moon** 1

Chapter 2 **Hunter Hysteria** 11

Chapter 3 **Hunter Heyday** 27

Chapter 4 **The Black Arrows** 59

Chapter 5 **The Blue Diamonds** 71

Chapter 6 **Home Thoughts From Abroad** 87

Index 151

FGA.9 XG261/'64' during a detachment to Karup, Denmark, 24–30 November 1973, when four Hunters of 45 Squadron took part in Exercise 'Ocean Span'. Some 6 in of snow fell and the temperature at one point plummeted to −18°C. The conditions were so bad that when the aircraft were taxiing from the iced-up dispersals an airman had to be placed on each wingtip to prevent the Hunter slipping sideways until some forward momentum had been built up. The discontinuity in the lower edge of the camouflage line and the presence of the camera window shows that this Hunter is using one of the 'Flying Camels'' interchangeable 'photo-noses'. (*Dave Ketteringham*)

Did I say low!

Acknowledgements

Thanks are due to the following individuals for their assistance in the creation of this book: George Aird; Alastair Aked; Tony Aldridge RAF (Retd); Brian Allchin RAF (Retd); Air Cdre G. 'Max' McA. Bacon RAF (Retd); Adrian Balch; Pat Barker; Chris Bassham; Alan Beaumont DPhil; Sqn Ldr Kenneth Becker RAF (Retd); Lawrence R. Bedford; Ian Bell, Tangmere Military Aviation Museum; Arthur Bennett; Roy Braybrook; Adrian Brown; Ken Bullard; Ian Cadwallader; Sqn Ldr Peter Carr RAF (Retd); Fred Cattermole; Ralph Chambers; Carole and Dennis Charlton; Bob Collis; Bob Cossey; Chris Cowper; Larry D'Eath; Wg Cdr R.J.F. 'Dickie' Dickinson RAF (Retd); Sqn Ldr Neville Duke DSO, OBE, DFC**, AFC Czech MC; Gp Capt Ed Durham RAF Retd; John Farley; Bern Flower; AVM Sam Goddard RAF (Retd); David Grimer; Val Grimble; Mike Haggerty; John Hale; Sheila Hamilton; Gp Capt Alan Hastings OBE; Eric G. Hayward; Ken Hazell; Gp Capt Mike Hobson CBE, AFC, RAF (Retd); Wg Cdr Gerry Honey OBE, RAF (Retd); M.J. Hornagold; Geoff Hurst; Roger Hymans RAF (Retd); Mick Jennings MBE; Ben Jones; David Jones; Dave Ketteringham; Terry Kingsley; Chris Lampard; Geoffrey H. Lee; Ted Liddell; Roger Mansfield; Philip Markham; Francis K. Mason BSc, FRHistS, FCGA, FACA, AMRAeS, RAF (Retd); Sqn Ldr Bernard J. Noble RAF (Retd); Alan Pollock; Wg Cdr Stuart G. Pountain RAF (Retd); François Prins; Brian Ralph; Laurie Reid; Bernard Reynolds; Paul Richardson; Richard D. Rix; AVM Boz Robinson RAF (Retd); Geoff Rosenbloom; Jack Rowe BEM; Bruce Rust; Graham Simons; Duncan Simpson OBE, CEng., FIMechE, FRAeS; Colin Smith; John Smith; Dave Stint; Vic A. Terry; Andy Thomas; Michael Thomas; Air Cdre Roger Topp AFC** RAF (Retd); Tom Trower; R. Twell; Tim Webb; Neal J. Wharton; Richard Wilson; and Andrew Woodroof. Special thanks go to Tony Aldridge for his unstinting help and advice, which included cross-checking the proofs on many occasions, and to Alison Flowers at Sutton Publishing for her diligence; she almost literally 'moved heaven and earth' to accommodate the very best photographs.

T.8 XF321 of the RAE over Farnborough in May 1973. This Blackpool-built F.4 was delivered to the RAF on 27 February 1956 and served with 130 Squadron before returning to Hawkers in 1958 for conversion to Hunter T.7 standard. It served with 56 and (from 1966) 8/43 Squadrons, before joining the RAE in 1976. (*Adrian Balch*)

T.7 XL619 of 45 Squadron at Machrihanish on 1 June 1973. This aircraft was flown for the first time on 7 January 1959 by David Lockspeiser and was delivered to the RAF on 3 February, serving with the Gütersloh Station Flight and subsequently with 20 Squadron. On 7 September 1972 XL619 joined 45 Squadron, moving to the Hunter Wing on 6 February 1975. On 28 July 1976 it joined the TWU at Brawdy and in 1979 moved to 2 TWU at Lossiemouth. (*Adrian Balch*)

CHAPTER 1

HUNTER'S MOON

British fighters had been among the world's finest during the Second World War. Many of them, such as the Hawker Hurricane and the Typhoon rocket-firing fighter, were the result of the design teams headed by Sydney Camm, who had been Hawker's chief designer since 1925. His greatest post-war creation, the Hunter, beckoned, but bringing this project (and others) to fruition would prove difficult. In 1945 Britain had emerged impoverished and austere from more than five years of war while the United States and the Soviet Union gained new dominance, both politically and militarily. British politicians tried forlornly to resuscitate and transform the economy but deprivation and sacrifice could not be remedied overnight, or even over a period of years. America gave Europe aid, but Britain's overall economic situation, certainly in the aviation industry, was one of under-investment and low priority. 'Make do and mend', an attitude reminiscent of the period immediately after the First World War, was the order of the day.

America had no such military aircraft replacement problems and her aviation industry, profiting hugely from captured data about secret German jet designs and advanced wing technologies, forged ahead with second-generation jet fighters and bombers. In Britain innovative design and aircraft production went largely unrewarded and remained under-funded. When the government did get involved, generally it was to meddle and confuse the situation. Fortunately, British aircraft designers and engine makers had lost none of their genius and invention – far from it. At their companies' expense, they began producing advanced commercial and military designs that would compete with, and in many cases beat, those of the rest of the world. The onset of the Cold War between East and West, with the Soviet blockade of Berlin in 1948 and the outbreak of war in Korea two years later, concentrated minds wonderfully on both sides of the Atlantic. (America would later fund production and deliveries of aircraft like the Hunter to nations outside the Communist Bloc.) Churchill and the Conservatives were returned to power in 1951 and the climate began to change from austerity to more sunlit uplands, whose warm glow lit up the design offices and production lines of Hawker, de Havilland, Gloster and Supermarine, to name but a few.

Actually, the change in direction had begun a few years before. 'Thank God for the Navy' Camm had written in August 1946. Once again the senior service provided the catalyst and much-needed salvation for Britain's post-war aircraft industry. On 27 July 1946 the first prototype

Supermarine Attacker flew at Chilbolton. A 1944 design earmarked originally for the RAF, in August 1951 it became the first jet aircraft to enter service with the Fleet Air Arm. By 1955 no piston-engined aircraft would be in first-line squadron service with the Royal Navy. In February 1946 an order was placed for three prototypes of Hawker's first jet fighter, the P.1040, which was adapted for carrier-based interception. The first P.1040 prototype flew at Boscombe Down, Wiltshire, on 2 September 1947. It was powered by a 4,500lb thrust Nene I, which produced a maximum speed of about Mach 0.77 (510mph). An increase in speed and performance only resulted when Camm forged ahead with plans for a swept-wing design, the P.1047, which was powered by a more powerful Nene engine. The new wings had a sweepback of 35 degrees on the quarter chord and a thickness ratio of 0.10.

In November 1946 Specification E.38/46 was issued by the Ministry of Supply (MoS) for two swept-wing examples, designated P.1052s, powered by the 5,000lb thrust Nene 2. The new design promised a maximum speed in excess of Mach 0.86 (560mph at 36,000ft) but in fact they proved capable of speeds up to Mach 0.90 (595mph at 36,000ft). All-swept tail surfaces and a straight-through jet-pipe helped improve the P.1052's performance and handling. But by the end of 1947 Camm and his design team knew that to overcome the lead set by Supermarine they would have to design a new aircraft, one that could accommodate the new 6,500lb Rolls-Royce A.J.65 axial-flow turbojet. This engine would soon become world famous as the Avon. The P.1052, meanwhile, went on to become the Sea Hawk, the first production F.1 flying in November 1951. Hawkers built just thirty-five Sea Hawks before full-scale production passed to Armstrong Whitworth Aircraft Ltd at Baginton, Coventry.

At Richmond Road in Kingston-upon-Thames, Hawker's main production plant, Camm now turned his attention to a new design derived from the P.1052 to meet Specification F.3/48, issued to Hawker early in 1948 for a single-seat, cannon armed, day interceptor/fighter powered by either a Rolls-Royce Avon or an Armstrong-Siddeley Sapphire engine. The new interceptor had to be capable of Mach 0.94 (620mph at 36,000ft, 724mph at sea level), and have an endurance of 60 minutes. No final decision had been made on the type of guns. They would be either four 20mm Hispano or two new 30mm Aden cannon. An ejection seat would be mandatory and provision had to be made for a future radar-ranging gunsight. The main characteristics of the original P.1067 design included an Avon engine mounted in the fuselage amidships, with an annular nose air intake and exhausting through a long jet-pipe in the extreme tail. The wing was swept back at 42½ degrees on the quarter chord and a straight-tapered tailplane was mounted on top of the fin (though this was deleted at the later P.1067/5 stage).

In 1949 the four 30mm Aden cannon armament fit was adopted, cleverly mounted with the magazines in a removable gun-pack located behind the cockpit. Though the German Me262 jet fighter of the Second World War had been armed with four cannon, and both the Gloster Javelin and the de Havilland DH.110 were being developed to include four Adens, the P.1067 was the only single-seat, single-engined fighter in the world designed to carry four cannon. In May 1950 the Ministry of Supply announced that the 30mm Aden would be abandoned because of cost considerations, but six weeks later changed its mind and decided to go with the original specification of four 30mm Aden cannon. Similarly, indecision initially surrounded the choice of the engine to power the P.1067. Hawker's chief rival, the Supermarine Swift, would be powered by the Rolls-Royce Avon, as would the English Electric Canberra twin-engined bomber. In the event, WB188, the first of the three P.1067 prototypes, and WB195, would be powered by the Avon, while the Sapphire would power WB202.

Work on the three prototypes continued throughout 1950 and 1951, and Hawker's chief test pilot, Sqn Ldr T.S. 'Wimpy' Wade, and his assistant, Sqn Ldr Neville Duke, waited in the wings to fly the first of the breed. Tragically, Wade was killed flying the P.1081 on 3 April 1951 and Duke was appointed chief test pilot. By

the end of June 1951 WB188 was almost ready for the first flight and it was painted with a glossy pale duck egg green finish to mark the occasion. On 27 June WB188 was dismantled at Kingston and transported to the Aeroplane and Armament Experimental Establishment at Boscombe Down, preparatory to the first flight. Neville Duke carried out WB188's first engine run on 1 July and on 20 July flew the prototype off the ground for a 47-minute flight. Two months later Duke was making high-speed passes in excess of 700mph at the Farnborough Air Show.

When Sqn Ldr Neville Duke (in cockpit) taxied out at Boscombe Down in the famous P.1067 Hunter prototype, WB188, on 20 July 1951 it would have looked just like this. This is in fact GA.11 WV256 (G-BZPB), painted in the same duck-egg green/sky paint scheme by Exeter-based Classic Jets to commemorate the event, fifty years later, at Boscombe Down. (*Adrian Balch*)

Opposite, inset: Armourers replenishing the Aden gun-pack from XG231/A of 92 Squadron in Cyprus in 1959. (*Brian Allchin*)

Opposite: Two 92 Squadron armourers hoisting up the Aden pack from its cradle into XG231/A using the Type C bomb hoist. Hawker Siddeley Aircraft purchased XG231 on 19 April 1966 for conversion to Jordanian F.6 (715), being delivered on 13 June 1967. (*Brian Allchin*)

Hunter Gun-Pack Change

'This was a three-man operation. One man to port, another to starboard and the man in charge at the front of the gun-pack. Each man had certain things to do: the front man removed two small panels from the front of the gun-pack, then unlocked and pulled the four gun barrels forward with the hockey stick. The port and starboard men removed the large rear panels where most of the links end up, then removed the "Sabrina" clips. (The clips on these panels were very much like the clips used to hold down the bonnet of a Triumph Herald.) One of the sidemen also had to screw the tail strut in.

'When all the panels and "Sabrinas" were off, the sidemen screwed a fishplate into either side of the aircraft. This is just a large bolt to hang the winch on. The front winch was attached to a strong point inside the aircraft and the hook was attached to a point on the front of the gun-pack. The side winches were attached to a wide strap which was wound up underneath the gun-pack. Then all three winches were cracked off, i.e. just like a torque spanner.

'The front man then made sure everything was ready: i.e. all barrels forward, tail strut in, power supply from aircraft to pack disconnected. On the command, "On Three – one, two three", everybody pressed the unlocking lever on the winch and slowly wound the pack down turning the handles anti-clockwise at all times and making sure the pack was coming down level on to the trolley. The barrels were withdrawn from the aircraft and placed two barrels either side of the trolley. Of course, a good team could drop a pack and replace another one in minutes. In fact, they used to race each other. The teams were not always all armourers. Sometimes the port and starboard men could be Airframe, Engine or any other trade but the front winch was always an armourer.

'If somebody forgot to screw the tail strut in once the pack was down, the centre of gravity altered and the aircraft gently sat down on the tailskid. But all you did was get a person to climb up on to the spine and work his way forward over the canopy and sit on the nose. Some aircraft sat lower down than others, which meant you couldn't screw a strut in. Then a heavy person had to sit in the cockpit during the change.

'When Hunters were doing aerobatics, i.e. 92 Squadron's Blue Diamonds, the ammo tank on top of the gun-pack was replaced by another tank to hold diesel to which a dye could be added for colour. The diesel was then pumped into the rear of the jet pipe creating smoke.'

Dennis Charlton

Watched by a 92 Squadron pilot, armourers lay out the 30mm Aden cannon shells on tabletops prior to loading them in the gun-packs. (*Brian Allchin*)

Sqn Ldr Neville Duke and WB188, now painted red overall and modified for the (successful) attempt on 7 September 1953 to break the World Absolute Air Speed Record. At this time WB188 was based at Tangmere, Sussex. (*HAL* via *François Prins*)

Sqn Ldr Neville Duke OBE, DSO, DFC**, AFC Czech, MC

'In 1951 I had to fly two aircraft at Farnborough, for "Wimpy" [Sqn Ldr T.S. Wade] had been killed in the P.1081 and there had been insufficient time to obtain another pilot, or for either Frank Murphy or Frank Bullen [company test pilots] to convert to the P.1052. I flew this aircraft, and also the P.1067 – the Hunter prototype. This was the best SBAC display I can recall. We felt that Hawkers had it all their own way on this occasion, for there was nothing to touch the P.1067 for speed or grace of line.

'One of the many interesting points about the 1952 Farnborough [show] was that, for the first time, the sonic boom or bang was produced regularly for the spectators . . . I have many memories of Farnborough, but those of 1952 will remain with me all my life. The death of John Derry and his observer, Tony Richards, together with the loss of twenty-eight spectators and the injury of many more was a great shock to everybody . . . Soon I had to stop thinking about them. It was time for me to go off, but there was a bit of a delay while the wreckage of the 110 was being cleared from the runway . . . It was a lovely day for flying. At 43,000ft over Odiham I could see the airfield clearly. While sitting up there at that height I had more time to spare and to think in the lonely world above the scattered cloud, in the clear visibility under the darkening canopy of the stratosphere.

'The cockpit was quiet and warm; everything was in first-class order. It would be untrue to say that I was not disturbed and worried by John's death. I reflected that so little is known of supersonic flight; perhaps it could have had something to do with the accident.

'Then it was time to dive. The Hunter did its stuff perfectly, the bangs were heard by the crowd at the display, and with that visibility, I should not have missed the mark . . . For me there is no greater satisfaction than sitting in the cockpit of a Hunter, beautiful in design and construction, representing the thought and skill of so many people, and feeling it respond to the slightest movement of your fingers. It lives and is obedient to your slightest wish. You have the sky to play in – a great limitless expanse . . .'

Extract from Neville Duke, Test Pilot (*Allan Wingate, 1953; rprt. Grub Street, 1992*)

'Neville Duke made the Hunter's maiden flight on 20 July 1951 and he played a vital part in the flight development programme. He deservedly hit the headlines with his stimulating Hunter demonstrations in the early 1950s, and by gaining the world speed record. Thus Neville and the Hunter became almost as synonymous as Sydney Camm and Hawker Aircraft Ltd were. It was my privilege to join Hawker as an Experimental Test Pilot under Neville in 1951, sharing the Hunter programme and taking over from him as chief test pilot from 1956 to 1967; thus the Hunter became an essential part of my life and one that I always reflect on with some pride and pleasure.'

Alfred William 'Bill' Bedford OBE, AFC, FRAeS (1920–96), writing in 1981

Bedford was Hawker's experimental test pilot when in August 1955 Neville Duke crash-landed a Hunter at Thorney Island after a gun-firing problem and damaged his back. On 9 May 1956 he exacerbated his back problem during a hard landing in the P.1099 and after many weeks of incapacity he had to resign in October 1956. Bill Bedford succeeded him as chief test pilot, serving in that role until 1968, when he became sales manager for Hawker Siddeley Aviation. Ten years later Bedford was appointed divisional marketing manager for BAe, a post he held until his retirement in 1983.

On 5 May 1952 Duke flew WB195, the second P.1067, now officially called the Hunter, from the new Hawker test field at Dunsfold in Surrey. WB195 had the same production RA (Reheated Avon) of 7,500lb thrust as WB188 but with variable swirl vanes, whereas the original Avon in WB188 had two position swirl vanes in the early flights. WB195 also had full military equipment, including four Aden cannon and radar-ranging gunsight. On 4 June Neville Duke put WB195 through its paces at West Raynham in front of the RAF's Central Fighter Establishment, which would be the first to receive production Hunters prior to their entry into squadron service. On 10 July 1952 Duke flew WB188 at the Brussels Air Show in front of a large and very appreciative crowd. The debut of the Hunter was eagerly anticipated at that year's SBAC show at Farnborough where WB195 was to be flown each day while WB188 was held in reserve. Sadly, the Hunter's triumphant debut here was overshadowed by the loss, on 6 September, of the de Havilland DH.110 prototype. The DH.110 broke up in the air as it turned towards the crowd line, killing pilot John Derry, his fellow crewmember Anthony Richards, and thirty people on the ground. A further sixty-three people were injured. Neville Duke was scheduled to display next in WB195 and in spite of the tragedy he carried on; he bravely took off and put on a truly brilliant flying display, which included a transonic dive.

Duke flew WB202, the third P.1067 prototype, for the first time on 30 November 1952 from Dunsfold. This prototype was powered by the Sapphire engine in place of the

---

'1952 was an auspicious year. Hawker Aircraft started getting contracts for the new Hunter fighter aircraft, but with their existing factory layouts had some difficulties in producing new orders. Their main production plant was at Richmond Road, Kingston, and the assembly and flight-testing factory was at Langley in Buckinghamshire. Hawkers found Langley airfield too close to the new London Airport and were offered, by the Ministry of Defence, Dunsfold in Surrey, which, being an ex-wartime airfield, had only two hangars and many old Nissen huts. Having agreed to the relocation, Hawkers secured their first Hunter production contract. They now had to find a large labour force to fulfil their obligation, and quickly. Hawkers had a major task on their hands. They had moved their complete final assembly shop, paint shop and delivery line to a new airfield over 30 miles away, then had to build a new group of hangars and final assembly shops, with all the associated infrastructure, and recruit a new labour force from the locals. I had an above-average interest in military jet fighter aircraft and I lived only 10 miles from Dunsfold at that time, so in January 1953 I applied to Hawkers. As my CV did not contain any previous aircraft experience I did not really expect a result. I carried on, tinkering with my second love, cars, motorbikes, etc., while working in the local garage as a mechanic. On 4 December Hawkers offered me, subject to interview, a job as a fitter/erector on a 44-hour week at the princely sum of 2s 9d an hour. An absolute fortune!

'When I arrived, the new three-bay production hangar was built, with the floor concrete in only two bays. The large paint shop was completed but not yet operating. (It could hold about five Hunters at any one time.) The two existing RAF hangars became the Spares Store and the Experimental Hangar. There was a selection of the pre-production Hunters (WT555 to 575) in the Erection Hangar. A few Sea Hawks and Sea Furies were dispatched by March 1954 leaving space for the production of the Mk I Hunters. By the beginning of 1954 production of the Mk I Hunters was coming along well with a steady flow of development in the main hangar.'

Eric Hayward

7,500lb thrust RA.7 and the aircraft went on to become the prototype Hunter F.2. (Hawker would build the Avon-powered F.1 at Kingston while Armstrong Whitworth at Coventry would build the Sapphire-engined Mk 2.) It was evident that they needed more than just three prototypes, and in effect the first twenty production Hunter F.1s would come to be regarded as development machines. These early Hunters were used to evaluate and test numerous trial installations, including an area-ruled fuselage, blown flaps and alternative styles of air brake. In 1952 WB188 had been fitted with 'clam shell' air brakes on the sides of the rear fuselage. A single ventral airbrake was ultimately selected and flight trials were made in 1953 to determine the best position for the brake to be located.

Other deficiencies early in service life included severe canopy misting after descending from high altitude, while air-firing trials identified a need to fit a housing to collect spent cartridge cases and links that might otherwise damage the airframe. Limited fuel capacity reduced the F.1's endurance substantially, and there was also the problem of rapid pitch-up, which began to occur without adequate warning in some manoeuvres at the higher subsonic Mach numbers. In addition there were severe compressor surge problems with the Avon 104, and to a lesser extent with the

'The question of fitting the airbrake posed a major problem. When produced as a prototype, the aircraft carried no airbrake, and this was a pretty slippery machine. Lowering the flaps slowed you up. It also changed the trim smartly. Anyway, the Ministry insisted that they would not accept the Hunter without an airbrake, even though we had started the production run. We then came up with the idea of fitting two lengths of Dexion angle bolted under the fuselage and this peculiar shovel-shaped thing with its hydraulic jack was moved backwards and forwards under the fuselage and flown to find the most effective position without altering the trim change greatly.

'Another persistent problem was vibration in the rudder area at certain speeds. Various tailplane fairings and shapes around the tailplane/fin juncture were tried; all with no real success, until one day one of the pilots spied in an aviation magazine an acorn fairing fitted to Russian aircraft. He said to the Design Office, "Why don't we try that?" They did and it cured it. (Perhaps they should have looked at the Westland Whirlwind fighter produced in wartime days.)

'With the introduction of a production line and subsequent flight testing, many mods and ideas were tried out. It was a very exciting time with many trial and error ideas being implemented. The undercarriage lock-up system was unsatisfactory and a major redesign of the system was carried out. Also, the flap balance gave trouble, which required a further major modification. The wiring used to make cable assemblies in the aircraft was found not to be resistant to the engine oil and became swollen and broke up when oil was spilt on them.

'The experimental hangar handled most of the development aircraft, WT555 to 575, but all production machines came through our main assembly line, although one DB aircraft, WT572, was in the Flight Shed for repairs. At that time the Hunter had no air brake and various trials and tests were being carried out to add this now accepted feature. 572's pilot [a NATO test pilot] had been told that flaps should be lowered as air brakes, with the result that a pipe burst in the hydraulic system and when he landed, the brakes would not stop him so he ran on to the overshoot. The damage was minimal but quite a lot of mud attached to the undercarriage of the aircraft. Later perforated flaps were fitted but this was found to be unsatisfactory also.'

Eric Hayward

Mk 113 engine. Engine surging noticeably increased when gun gases were ingested during high altitude gun-firing. Diving to increase airspeed and to reduce altitude usually effected recovery from the surge but engine flame-out often resulted. Various remedies were tried to rid the Avon of these problems but they were only finally eliminated with the introduction of the surge-free RA 21. The 8,000lb thrust Sapphire 101-powered Hunter F.2, however, had no such engine surge problems and gun-firing was cleared up to 47,000ft. Also, the Sapphire, as fitted to the F.2, could develop slightly more thrust at a lower specific fuel consumption than could the Avon as fitted to the F.1. It is all the more surprising therefore, that Rolls-Royce gained the lion's share of Hunter engine allocation. Avon engines powered all the Hunters in service except for 105 F.5s which were Sapphire-powered. Frank Murphy flew WT555,

the first production Hunter F.1, at Dunsfold on 16 May 1953, but the F.1 would not finally enter service until late in July 1954.

Meanwhile, in 1953 WB188 was modified for an attempt to break the World Absolute Air Speed Record, which then stood at 715.75mph. This had been set by Lt Col William F. Barnes on 16 July 1953 in a North American F-86D Sabre. In August that year WB188 was adapted to take an RA 7R Avon capable of 7,130lb thrust 'dry' and 9,600lb with reheat lit. The Hunter, which was painted bright red overall and designated the Mk 3, also received a sharply pointed nose-cone fairing and a windscreen fairing giving reduced wind resistance. The latter was deleted after the record flights. As Neville Duke remembers, 'We experienced misting up between it and the "real" windscreen during subsequent test flights at altitude.'

Operating from Tangmere in Sussex, on 7 September Neville Duke made one practice run

---

'Unfortunately, no aircraft is perfect first time. Only after many hours of flight testing, delivery and service use do the bugs start to come out. The art then is to find out the cause and cure the problem as soon as possible. Dunsfold and its labour force were masters of this. A good illustration of snags appearing unexpectedly was on 7 July 1954, when, having our first batch of Hunter Mk 1s ready for delivery, a ceremony was arranged when four pilots from 43 Squadron (Leuchars) arrived to collect the aircraft. VIPs, the Press and TV were all present. It was a beautiful hot July day. Speeches were made, hand-over documents presented, toasts were drunk and all went splendidly, with much self-congratulation. On the apron stood four magnificent, gleaming new Hunters, WT580, 582, 584 and 585. A passing thunderstorm with a deluge of heavy rain halted proceedings momentarily. However, it soon cleared, and out walked the four pilots, somewhat reminiscent of the Formula 1 start line, but with more dignity, to climb into their bright shiny new machines. At the given signal, all fired their starter cartridges with military precision. All engines were running, the Press rushing about shooting their cameras. Microphones were at the ready to hear that magnificent roar. All appeared to be well. Not so, all the engines were shut down. Pilots disembarked and they rejected the aircraft. Many in the crowd muttered, wondering what was amiss. The pilots too were muttering in true pilot fashion when things do not go to plan, and I heard the words, "No JPT [jet-pipe temperature] readings". Critical examination revealed that rainwater from the summer storm had run into the rear fuselages, soaked the asbestos-covered thermocouple cables and shorted out the readings. A valuable lesson was learned. From this point on all JPT cables were sheathed with PVC. All the aircraft departed satisfactorily the following day, but the kudos of the initial launch had been lost somewhat.'

Eric Hayward

'I was privileged to see how a good test pilot reacts in an emergency. Bill Bedford was flying WT557 on test on 12 August 1954 when, on selecting undercarriage "down" his legs failed to lower. It was evening and so we were stopped on our way home in our cars at the runway threshold. So all we could do was sit there and watch the incident happen. He elected to belly-land alongside the runway [and he] floated in, touched down and slithered on his belly along the grass until the aircraft stopped. As we watched, the flaps were retracted, one wing tip gently touched the ground and then the engine was shut down. The cockpit canopy slid open and out climbed Bill, minus cockpit ladder. Damage was minimal and the aircraft was later jacked-up, the defects rectified and back on flight-test two days later. A truly professional pilot at work!'

Eric Hayward

'If ever there was a real pilot's aeroplane it was the Hunter but, like any worthwhile project, it had its fair share of teething troubles before it emerged as a winner. Problems were experienced with buffeting at high speed, longitudinal control, radio reliability, demisting, pitch-up, gun-firing, air brakes, engine surge and the like. Their solution extended the ingenuity of the Hawker team but they were to be the making of an outstanding multi-purpose combat aircraft. It excelled in the roles of interceptor fighter, ground attack, reconnaissance, research vehicle and two-seater trainer, not forgetting the dramatic formation aerobatic performances . . . For three decades pilots have enthused about the beautiful Hunter with its smooth aerodynamic lines, four 30mm cannon, the Rolls-Royce Avon engine, outstandingly honest handling characteristics combined with a lively performance. It was undoubtedly a classic thoroughbred of its time from the stables of one of the finest fighter manufacturers in the world.'

Alfred William 'Bill' Bedford, OBE, AFC, FRAeS, writing in 1981

and two timed record runs in WB188 along the 3km course off the coast near Rustington. The final run was 727.63, a Mach number of approximately .95. On 19 September Duke flew WB188 round a 100km closed circuit to set a new world record for this course at 709.2mph.

Shortly afterwards the Supermarine Swift broke Duke's speed record, flying at 735.70mph in Libya where higher ambient temperatures greatly assisted the record-breaking attempt. 'Had we gone to Libya,' recalls Neville Duke, 'the Hunter would have achieved about 750mph.'

CHAPTER 2
HUNTER HYSTERIA

The Hunter Enters RAF Service

'In January 1954 the Swift and the Hunter were eagerly awaited at the Central Fighter Establishment at RAF West Raynham. At that time I was serving as a pilot on the Air Fighting Development Squadron, the unit responsible for carrying out operational trials on new fighter aircraft. The Swift arrived in January 1954, but the Hunter F.1 was delayed for the fitting of an airbrake under the rear fuselage. The original idea of using underwing flaps as air brakes, as on the Swift, had proved unsatisfactory due to the strong nose down trim change on extending. Eventually, on 5 July, three modified Hunters were ready at Dunsfold. Sqn Ldr Seaton, Flt Lt Calvey and I went down to collect them. After a brief lunch and a short briefing, we climbed aboard, took off and flew direct to West Raynham, passing over London en route (as one did in those days). On arrival we were met by the Commandant, who congratulated us for getting three Hunters in the air at the same time!

'After acceptance checks and a few familiarisation flights we were pitched in to the Fighter Command Exercise on 18 July. This was carried out in appalling weather. The Hunter gave a good account of itself but several deficiences on the Mk 1 aeroplane came to light. Fuel shortage was a main concern, particularly in the weather prevailing. Inevitable radio and severe cockpit canopy icing and misting added to this. However, my logbook records thirteen sorties, mostly as "wing-man" to my CO, Wg Cdr Bird-Wilson. A variety of "enemy" aircraft were intercepted, including Canberras. B-47s, B-45s and Sabres. There was no doubt that the Hunter, with its initial shortcomings rectified, was going to be a really successful aeroplane. It was fast, had a good rate of climb and handled well. There were still problems associated with the Rolls-Royce Avon engine, particularly at high altitude and when firing the four 30mm Aden guns.

'The trials continued and we learned more about the Hunter's capabilities and deficiences. Comparative trials were made with our own Venoms and F-86 Sabres. In October the Development Squadron received its first Mk 2 Hunters, very similar to the Mk 1 in terms of equipment, but fitted with the Armstrong Siddeley Sapphire engine. The Sapphire in fact perfomed at altitude slightly better than the Avon, and was less prone to engine surge, particularly during gun firing. I made only two flights on the Hunter Mk 2 before leaving the RAF to join Hawker Aircraft at Dunsfold. On arrival at Hawkers I was immediately put to work on production testing the remaining Hunter Mk 1s off the line and the later Mk 4, which had extra internal fuel.

'In October 1955 the first Mk 6 Hunters came on production test – a quantum leap in performance when the aircraft was fitted with the 10,000lb thrust Rolls-Royce 200 Series Avon engine. Apart from some initial blade and other teething problems the Hunter and Avon were developed into the finest and most robust fighter airframe/engine combinations in the shape of the developed Mk 9.

'The Hunter very quickly began to sell and eventually saw service in some twenty countries in single and two-seat form. In many cases, notably in Switzerland, it was selected against some formidable opposition.

'The Hunter was everyone's favourite!'

Duncan Simpson, OBE, C. Eng, FIMechE, FRAeS, Hawker test pilot (1954–78)

Duncan Simpson, Hawker test pilot from 1954 to 1978. He is seen here in the cockpit of G-BABM (previously FGA.9 XF432, repurchased by HAS as G-9-363 and becoming an FR.74B for Singapore, No. 526), resplendent in desert camouflage and displaying the flags of eighteen countries that bought the Hunter.
G-BABM appeared at the 1976 Farnborough Air Show. (*Duncan Simpson*)

F.1 WT594, one of the first production batch of 113 aircraft built by Hawkers at Kingston, flew for the first time on 2 July 1954 with Frank Bullen at the controls. It was delivered to 5 MU on 17 September 1954 and was issued to 43 Squadron. (via *GMS*)

'There has been a tendency to bestow a personality upon the machine; this is only really credible when bestowed by the men who built and flew it. The Hunter has been a long-serving and faithful workhorse, a beast admired and respected by most, and perhaps hated by a few. It certainly had its tribulations in its early days, now almost forgotten, but these were overcome – they had to be, for after the disastrous eclipse of the Supermarine Swift, the Hunter was the only British fighter on the horizon.

'Certainly as time passed this very beautiful aeroplane began to acquire a kind of charisma. It was as if the meticulous design treatment by the dedicated team, led by a man who possessed a unique appreciation of beauty and grace in the flying machine, was being reflected in the behaviour of the Hunter. The pilots quickly learned how to get the best from their aeroplanes and became their staunch advocates. And long after individual aircraft had passed their predicted fatigue life (the 'three-score years and ten' of the aeroplane), Hunters were being painstakingly refurbished and sent into the air again. There are numerous instances in which individual Hunters have flown with three or four different air forces of the world, and at least one has flown with no fewer than seven! Little wonder that something of a mystique can be detected in the "character" of the Hunter. In at least one air force Hunters served for almost fifty years before being finally retired. Unquestionably this will not be matched by any other front-line aeroplane in history.'

Francis K. Mason

On 1 July 1954 the Hunter F.1 was issued with a limited CA Release to enable the type to be flown by the Central Fighter Establishment (CFE) at West Raynham, which received about twelve newly modified Hunters early that same month. In addition, 43 Squadron at RAF Leuchars in Scotland began receiving its first Hunter F.1s, becoming fully operational by October. Late in 1954, 257 and 263 Squadrons at Wattisham began receiving Hunter F.2s, while 222 Squadron, also at Leuchars, received F.1s in December 1954. In February 1955, 54 Squadron at Odiham in Hampshire became the third and last first-line Hunter F.1 unit. The engine surge problems associated with the F.1 restricted all other deliveries to 229 and 233 Operational Conversion Units (OCUs), based at Chivenor in Devon and Pembrey near Llanelli respectively. No. 229 OCU, previously a Vampire and then a Sabre conversion unit, began receiving the Hunter in April 1955, and the first Hunter conversion course began on 15 May.

The year 1955 was also memorable in that it saw the appearance of the first official four-man Hunter aerobatic display team, 54 Squadron's Black Knights. (No. 43 Squadron had an unofficial three-man team in 1954, called the Fighting Cocks after the cockerel on the squadron crest, but this became an official Fighter Command four-man team in 1956.) Capt Richard G. 'Dick' Immig of Gillette, New Jersey, a 6ft-tall USAF exchange pilot with a crew-cut, who was OC B Flight, had done some aerobatic flying in the US. While they were

F.4 WV326 formerly of 74 'Tiger' Squadron, pictured at RAF Halton on 7 May 1971 when it was used as a ground instructional airframe (7669M). This aircraft was flown for the first time on 7 June 1955 by Frank Bullen and first served with 54 Squadron before joining the 'Tigers'. In January 1972 WV326 was flown back to Hawkers and converted to FR.71A (J735) for the Chilean Air Force, who received it on 11 January 1974. (*Adrian Balch*)

talking about it one day, one of his pilots, Flg Off P.V.L. 'Pete' Hamilton, asked Immig to set up an unofficial aerobatic team. Immig, who had flown a combat tour in Korea, was not over-enthusiastic, mainly because at the time the squadron was equipped with the Meteor F.8, but he was finally persuaded in October 1954 to ask for official permission for three of them to form up. 'I don't think you'll kill yourselves,' said their wing commander. 'Go ahead.' Immig expected the Hunter, when it arrived, to be a good aircraft for formation aerobatics.

In February 1955, 54 Squadron received its first Hunter F.1, with the remaining fifteen aircraft following in short order. Conversion flying started early in March, and by the end of the month virtually all the squadron pilots had completed their ten conversion trips. There was no dual-control trainer version at this time. Team practice started during the latter part of April when the pilots had each amassed about 15 hours on type. Flg Off P.A. 'Pat' Swoffer, the No. 3 man, now became reserve man of the team and Flg Off Bernard 'Nobby' Noble moved into his position. Noble recalls:

> Our early experience confirmed the Hunter to be a good aircraft for formation aerobatics. It had plenty of power and very good flying controls with powerful ailerons, and a tailplane which was trimmed by operation of a thumb switch on the stick. Manoeuvrability at all speeds was very good, and it had no apparent vices. In short, it met all the requirements. At the time there was no official Fighter Command aerobatic team, so it was an opportune moment to create one using the latest type of fighter to enter service.

By now the three-man team – all from B Flight – had become fairly proficient and they asked to be allowed a fourth man in the box position. It was Immig who made the official approaches – on condition that if he succeeded the rest of the team would have crew-cuts. On 10 May 11 Group's

Senior Air Staff Officer (SASO) visited Odiham to see them flying as a quartet for the first time. They passed the test. 'It meant', Immig recalls, 'that we were a real team. I took the boys over to Greenham Common, the USAF base, and got each of them a crew-cut.' Flg Off Colin J. 'Chunky' Redhouse became the No. 4 man.

During the following months the team carried out twenty-one official displays, as well as numerous practices. They included performances at Metz in France and at Geneva in Switzerland, where, in a moment of verbal inspiration, the French radio commentator labelled the Odiham team '*les Flêches Volantes*' ('the Flying Arrows'). They also flew on five days at Farnborough in September. Colin Redhouse left the service on completion of his Short Service Commission that same month, and Plt Off K.R. 'Curt' Curtis, who had recently joined A Flight, took his place. Curt, a Canadian, was an experienced pilot who had completed a tour as an instructor on Meteors before being commissioned. At about the same time the Hunter F.1 was replaced by the very similar F.4, the main difference being that the latter carried an additional 80 gallons of fuel in the wings. At Farnborough in 1955 a service unit appeared for the very first time in the UK's most glittering commercial show. For general performances like this the team worked out a programme designed to appeal to the general public – a programme that Immig described as 'low, tight and noisy'. Unfortunately, for reasons that will become apparent, less than two months later the Black Knights had ceased to exist.

Flg Off Bernard 'Nobby' Noble recalls the last flight of 54 Squadron's aerobatic team:

> To round off the season, Dick Immig arranged for a USAF photographer and a photographer from Independent Television (ITV) to visit Odiham on 3 November to record the team in action. It was agreed that the USAF photographer would fly with Pat Swoffer in the 54 Squadron Vampire T.11 whilst

F.4 WW641/B, F.1 WT659/U, and 'P' and 'K' of 54 Squadron's Black Knights, pictured at Farnborough on 9 July 1955. (via *Adrian Balch*)

the ITV man would fly with Flt Lt Bob Bragg in the navigator's seat of a Meteor NF.14 night fighter of 46 Squadron.

At this time the Odiham Air Traffic Control (ATC) Cathode Ray Direction Finder (CRDF), which provided instantaneous bearing on any aircraft transmitting on the radio approach frequency, had a long-standing fault and reliance had to be placed on a manual direction finder (D/F). The CRDF was used to home aircraft to the airfield and also to control them during the descent before handing over to the Ground Controlled Approach (GCA) radar. The manual D/F required the pilot to give a reasonably long transmission to allow the operator to swing his loop aerial on to the aircraft bearing, and this slowed aircraft handling; it also gave the possibility of mistakes if the operator was under pressure. Rapid handling was important with aircraft needing to be fed on to the GCA, either singly or in pairs, at two-minute intervals. However, the Royal Aircraft Establishment (RAE) at Farnborough lay only about 6 miles to the east of

Odiham. Their ATC had good radar coverage over the area, and, as experimental flying was limited in poor weather, they were able to offer a service whereby Odiham ATC kept them informed of the situation, so that aircraft overshooting from an approach at Odiham could be picked up and given a radar-controlled approach on to the runway at Farnborough. To enable Farnborough radar to make a rapid identification, this procedure depended upon the aircraft being overhead or very near to Odiham at the time; if it was not, the pilot had to obtain a homing back to Odiham.

The weather over southern England on the morning of 3 November was poor, with a cloud base of 300ft in drizzle and cloud tops at 5,000ft with no improvement forecast. Under these conditions Dick decided to go ahead with the flight, depending on the Farnborough overshoot procedure to cover any problems caused by the lack of CRDF at Odiham. The team took off in pairs; I was leading the second pair, and the photographic aircraft followed individually, but we all soon joined up above cloud for the photographic session. A considerable amount of time was then spent in photographing the aerobatics, and in so doing we drifted quite a long way from base. Pat Swoffer was the first to call that he was down to minimum fuel, and to break off and head for home, with the rest of us following shortly afterwards. The result was that all six aircraft arrived back in the Odiham area at approximately the same time, and all running short of fuel.

At this stage the D/F operator seemed to be coping satisfactorily. Pat Swoffer was first to let down for a controlled descent and GCA, while I followed with Curt on my wing two minutes later as we had less fuel than the lead pair. There was a light easterly wind, and after homing to overhead Odiham we were let down to the west with the intention of turning back towards the east before being picked up by the GCA for a talkdown on to runway 10. It would seem that things got out of hand at this stage as neither Pat in the Vampire nor Curt and I were lined up sufficiently accurately to be picked up by the Odiham GCA. Finally Odiham ATC told Pat to call Farnborough for a radar approach and landing there, and we received the same instruction about two minutes later. By this time we must have been to the east of Odiham, and the Farnborough Radar Controller was unable to identify either the Vampire or our Hunters. First he advised Pat to return to overhead Odiham so that he could be identified and given a radar approach into Farnborough. This was not possible as Pat had insufficient fuel, so the Controller tried to carry out a radar identification, but when Pat said that he was virtually out of fuel all the Controller could do was to tell him to pull up and bale out. With his remaining fuel Pat climbed above the cloud and jettisoned the cockpit canopy. Then, as it was an early model T.11 without ejection seats, he rolled the aircraft inverted so that first the USAF photographer, and then he, could drop out and open their parachutes. Both landed without injury. Apparently this was the American photographer's first flight, and it must have been a frightening experience for him to bale out under difficult circumstances.

Meanwhile Curt and I were flying on a south-easterly heading at a speed of 220 knots at 2,000ft in thick cloud when I first called Farnborough, and heard Pat's last transmissions. Bill Pendrey was the Farnborough Radar Controller, and he remained completely calm while telling Pat to pull up and bale out. He then tried to help us and, when that was not possible, told us to pull up and eject. I then called Curt to tell him to increase power for the climb; he acknowledged and suggested that we make a Mayday call on the distress frequency, but we barely had time to change frequency before he said something else, which I could not distinguish. I immediately looked round but his aircraft had already disappeared in the thick cloud as his engine flamed-out through lack of fuel. [WT709 crashed at Slinfold in Sussex.] He subsequently made a safe ejection and descent by parachute. To enable the Distress Services to get a fix on our position I made a Mayday transmission as I climbed into the clear air, expecting to have to eject.

Both Biggin Hill ATC and Tangmere ATC replied immediately, and as my Distance Measuring Equipment (DME) was locked on to the Tangmere beacon and indicated a range of 15 miles, I called Tangmere. Sqn Ldr John Jarvis, the Senior ATC Officer, immediately replied with a course to steer for Tangmere. This placed me to the north-east of Tangmere, and having levelled out in clear air at 7,000ft I realised that I would be able to reach Tangmere even if the engine stopped. When John Jarvis reported the cloud base at Tangmere was 800ft I decided to attempt a forced landing there, with the option of ejecting if this did not work out. With both fuel gauges just about on zero, I closed the throttle and decided not to rely on engine power any further. As I was then obviously fairly close to Tangmere I pushed the nose down till the speed built up to 350 knots. This gave me plenty of speed after breaking cloud either to land at Tangmere, or to pull up and eject if this was not possible. Tangmere gave headings to steer each time I transmitted and I must have passed just north of them on a westerly heading before breaking cloud in a left turn over Chichester, and immediately recognizing where I was. Still turning hard left the aircraft was travelling very fast and I realised that it would not be possible to land on the main runway. Undercarriage and full flap were hastily lowered and I was then able to line up for touch-down on the grass to the north side of the runway, and parallel to it.

The touch-down was firm and somewhat above the correct speed, and the braking action on the grass was poor so, as the aircraft was heading straight towards some concrete blast pens on the far side of the airfield, the undercarriage was selected up. The undercarriage came up immediately and the aircraft began porpoising along on its belly. Fortunately I had tightened my straps as it was a very rough ride, but eventually the aircraft turned round and stopped well short of the blast pens. I was very relieved to be still in one piece, especially as I had been airborne for a total of 70 minutes. This must have constituted some sort of record for the Hunter 4 without underwing tanks, especially as we had not been above 15,000ft. The first person on the spot as I clambered out was the Station Commander, Johnny Kent, who happened to have been driving his car round the airfield perimeter track. Fortunately, we were well acquainted, as he had previously been Station Commander at Odiham. He had had a distinguished career during the Battle of Britain and later as a fighter leader during the war, and obviously knew how to handle situations such as this. After I had given him a brief explanation of the reason for this unseemly arrival on his airfield, he looked at his watch and said "It's 11 o'clock, let's go and open the bar!" A brief visit was paid to the ATC tower so that I could thank John Jarvis for getting me out of trouble. Then, after a couple of drinks, and lunch, I was provided with a car to take me back to Odiham. The following day Pat, Curt and I reported to the Cambridge military hospital at Aldershot for back X-rays and other tests; fortunately we were all completely fit. [WT721 was subsequently repaired and modified to GA.11 standard before issue to the RN Fleet Requirements Unit.]

Meanwhile, Dick and Pete began their descent for Odiham two minutes behind Curt and myself, and the D/F operator lined them up sufficiently well for the GCA controller to pick them up, but he was not able to get them lined up on the runway. Nevertheless Bill Pendrey was able to identify them as they overshot from Odiham and gave them a very quick radar approach to land on runway 07 at Farnborough where two very relieved officers touched down with little fuel remaining. By this time Bob Bragg in the Meteor was flying on one engine to conserve fuel. He had an additional problem in that he did not believe that his photographer would bale out if the time came, so he was forced to let down simply on D/F headings. Fortunately he eventually broke through the low cloud safely, and was able to land at Odiham, the only aircraft to make it back.

F.4 XF302 formerly of 43 Squadron at Halton on 7 May 1971, when it was used as ground instructional airframe 7774M. Originally it had been delivered to the RAF on 30 December 1955. On 16 December 1971 XF302 was returned to Armstrong Whitworth Aircraft at Baginton for conversion to FGA.71, and once rebuilt was delivered to the Chilean Air Force (as J-733) on 15 February 1974. (*Adrian Balch*)

In retrospect it was an ill-conceived venture, given the weather conditions and the paucity of approach aids at Odiham. Having decided to fly, we should have returned to Odiham with sufficient fuel to cater for the ATC problems, but this we failed to do. The only redeeming features of the whole sorry affair, which resulted in the destruction of the Vampire and one Hunter with damage to another, was that no one was hurt, and there was absolutely no panic. Apart from the failure of the Odiham ATC system, which was perhaps understandable in the circumstances, once the situation developed everyone did what was expected of them, there was no panic and we were lucky. Following a Board of Inquiry the Wg Cdr Flying and the Sqn Cdr were posted, and Dick Immig was interviewed by the AOC 11 Group. There was also a general tightening up of the rules covering many aspects of Fighter Operations and of aerobatic teams in particular.

Only two people came out of this accident with much credit. Pat Swoffer did exceptionally well to get his American photographer, who had never flown before, to bale out, but he received no commendation for this. Perhaps the Board of Inquiry considered that, as captain of an individual aircraft, he should have returned to base with a sufficient fuel reserve to carry out a second approach in case he missed on the first, and that this ruled out any commendation for his subsequent good show. On the ATC side, Bill Pendrey was plunged into an impossible situation when Odiham ATC handed the Vampire and the first pair of Hunters to him without any prior warning. Nevertheless, he remained calm, and rapidly assessed the situation before advising the pilots to pull up and bale out. For the second pair of Hunters he was presented with very difficult circumstances. Both aircraft were very short of fuel, at close range and well off the extended centre line of the Farnborough runway when he took control, but he managed to get them in. He received a letter of commendation from the AOC 11 Group, AVM H.L. Patch, for saving the second pair of Hunters, but no mention was made of his efforts to help the Vampire and the first pair.

It was a sad end to the aerobatic team.

Four months later there was another disaster. 'Riddle of the Hunters: OUT OF FUEL JETS CRASH SIX IN A ROW', announced the *Daily Mail* on the morning of Thursday 9 February 1956. The day

> 'The morning of 8 February 1956 was a damp, dismal, day with very poor visibility. We should have moved GCA but it was broken down and unable to operate. So, we didn't expect any flying and were surprised when eight Hunters of DFLS took off. We waited for them to return for refuelling. Then, at approximately 11.30 panic broke out on the camp. There was no means of bringing them in under such bad conditions.'
>
> *R. Twell, civilian refueller driver, RAF Marham*

before, six Hunter F.1s of the Day Fighter Leaders' School (DFLS) at RAF West Raynham had crashed out of fuel and in bad weather while trying to land.

Wednesday 8 February 1956 had dawned overcast and misty. In North Sea areas such poor weather conditions could roll in very quickly. Eight pilots of the DFLS – six students and two staff pilots – were briefed for a 4-vs.-4 dogfight in their Hunter F.1s. By late morning the weather had cleared sufficiently to allow the formation to take off. One by one the Hunters flew into cloud at 450ft. At 11,000ft they broke out into brilliant sunshine where they completed their dogfights before returning overhead the station at 20,000ft. By now the weather at West Raynham had deteriorated and it was decided to divert the Hunters to RAF Marham, 15 miles distant. They left the West Raynham overhead at 2,000ft in cloud at 20-second intervals but the spacing between sections was too close to effect a safe talk-down at Marham and the F.1s, with dwindling fuel reserves, were forced to overshoot into the GCA pattern. The first pair broke cloud at 500ft and the leader managed to land from a low-level visual circuit. His No. 2, after his third timed circuit, was also able to land, his engine flaming-out on the runway.

The second pair, Lt Cdr Neville Williams RN in WT639/N and Sqn Ldr Richard Tumility in WW635/L, descended to 500ft but failed to break out of cloud. Williams safely ejected when his engine flamed-out and his Hunter crashed in a field at Beechamwell, boring a hole 12ft deep in the ground just 300 yards from an isolated farmhouse. Sadly, thirty-year-old Sqn Ldr Tumility was killed when his aircraft, the canopy already jettisoned, crashed in a field at Great Fransham.

As the third pair, Flt Lt B. Watford in WW603/G ('Yellow 1') and staff instructor Flt Lt J. McPherson in WW633/H ('Yellow 2'), reached Marham they were cleared down to 600ft, but had to descend to 250ft to break cloud. These two Hunters became separated and, with just 12 gallons of fuel remaining, McPherson climbed to 2,000ft and ejected. His Hunter crashed in a ploughed field opposite the Narborough–Narford road. Watford, meanwhile, was circling below cloud at 150ft attempting to locate the airfield and had to climb to avoid tall trees. Descending again to 150ft, he managed to find the runway but on turning finals his engine flamed-out through fuel shortage. Too low to

> 'After this latest incident urgent mod programmes were following through which resulted in the Hunter Mk 4. Basically [it was] the same aircraft with internal wing tanks and underwing inboard pylons to carry 100 gallon drop-tanks. Later Mk 4s also had outboard pylons, which gave a total tankage of 814 gallons, a massive step forward. So, as the Mk 4s came through on the production lines they rapidly replaced the earlier Mk Is, which were relegated to 229 OCU at Chivenor and 233 OCU Pembrey.'
>
> *Eric Hayward*

eject, Watford force-landed straight ahead, finishing up in a hedge beside the road at Barton Bendish. He was unhurt, and although the Hunter was not seriously damaged it never flew again.

The last pair consisted of 34-year-old Sqn Ldr W. Ives in WT629/T ('Red 3') and 25-year-old Flt Lt Mike Norman in WW639/X ('Red 4'). They overflew Marham with heavy R/T congestion and set up for a GCA but Marham had difficulty picking them up, so they descended

> 'I was the engineer officer on 67 Squadron, which together with 71, 112 and 130 Squadrons formed the Brüggen Wing of 2nd TAF and converted from Sabres to Hunters shortly before I was posted to 229 OCU. It became one of my happiest and interesting tours in the service, working with a wonderful aircraft. No. 229 OCU trained pilots, many of them Iraqis, from several countries that had bought the Hunter. One of my duties was to give them the technical lectures and I often wondered how much of their instruction managed to pierce the language barrier. One of the RAF pilot instructors remarked that some of the foreign trainees could quote verbatim from the manuals, but seemed to have little idea of what was actually meant and were incapable of applying the knowledge in a simulated emergency. Not all were like that. An Indian squadron leader, a striking looking Sikh with his beard and turban, had a port undercarriage hang up. ATC gave the crash alert over the Tannoy: pilots tore out of the crewroom, leapt into cockpits of aircraft on the line and taxied rapidly out of possible harm's way. The chaps in the ATC runway caravan were not so sharp. They evacuated the caravan but remained close by it to watch the fun. The pilot made a greaser of a landing but, inevitably, the port wing eventually dipped to the ground and the Hunter slewed in an anti-clockwise turn. As a result, the starboard wing was turning at quite a rate towards the airmen near the caravan, who tried to beat Olympic sprint records. Those of us watching from a safe distance saw that all but one had made it. He went down as though pole-axed and we thought the wing had hit his skull. It turned out that the wing had just cleared him but he had fainted from shock. After all that, the Sikh pilot climbed out of the cockpit as cool as a cucumber, apparently unperturbed by the whole thing. Best of all, the damage to the Hunter was not severe.'
>
> *Wg Cdr Stuart G. Pountain, engineer officer, 229 OCU, RAF Chivenor, December 1956–April 1959*

to 600ft where both were still in cloud. As they climbed past 2,500ft, the two became separated. Norman's engine flamed-out and he ejected, landing safely. After a search in the fog which blanketed the area, Watton Fire Brigade found the remains of the Hunter on the edge of a wood near the Stoke Ferry road at Cockley Cley. It had crashed beside a field in which two men were ploughing in tractors. Norman walked across to his crashed Hunter and was taken to the Cockley Cley estate office on the back of one of the tractors. Ives, meanwhile, had climbed to 4,000ft and also ejected. (He had survived a similar hair-raising experience a week earlier when he ran short of fuel on a diversion, landing in a snow shower with 25 gallons of fuel on a runway lit with flares!) Like Norman, Ives landed safely and the Hunter crashed in a field at Great Thornes Farm, Swaffham.

The first aircraft had landed at 1132 hr and the last crashed just 8 minutes later. A long period of bad weather ensued and flying did not resume until 28 February. Replacement aircraft began to arrive the following month when four Hunters were flown in from RAF Leuchars.

Training aircrew for Hunter operations became so important that 233 OCU was formed at Pembrey in 1956. The only other units to use the Hunter F.1 and F.2 were the Empire Test Pilots School (ETPS) at RAE Farnborough and the Fighter Weapons School at Leconfield, Yorkshire. Hawker Aircraft at Kingston built 113 Hunter F.1s altogether, while a second production batch of 26 aircraft was built by Hawkers at Blackpool. Armstrong Whitworth at Coventry built just 45 F.2s before production switched to the F.4.

The P.1101 trainer prototype (XJ615) flew for the first time on 8 July 1955. This two-seater was

The first two-seat prototype P.1101 XJ615 at Farnborough on 11 September 1959. This aircraft, powered by a Rolls-Royce Avon RA 21 engine, was flown for the first time on 8 July 1955 at Dunsfold by Neville Duke. Initially, it was armed with two Aden cannon but one gun was later deleted. XJ615 was used on numerous trials including hood development, spinning and gun firing. (*Tom Trower*)

Taking the Hunter for a Spin

Having graduated from No. 15 Course at the ETPS at Farnborough in December 1956, Flt Lt Bernard Noble was posted to A Squadron at Boscombe Down where he spent three very happy years flying fighters and trainers, plus anything else he could lay his hands on. One of the more interesting trials in which he was involved was Hunter spinning:

'Spinning trials were carried out in the early days on the Hunter, and these showed that the standard spin recovery technique of full opposite rudder and stick fully forward was reliable and effective, provided that the ailerons were held neutral. If more than a small amount of outspin aileron (against the direction of spin) was applied, the aircraft would not recover, so to assist the pilot in centralising the ailerons a white disc was painted on the instrument panel for him to aim at when moving the stick forward. Information on the spin and recovery was included in Pilots' Notes, although service pilots were prohibited from intentional spinning. No problems were recorded during the Hunter's early days in service but, with the increasing numbers of aircraft, difficulties arose in 1956. Several pilots got into spins, and a number ejected, and it was thought that the extended leading edges fitted to the outboard wing section made the aircraft more prone to spin. In those days it was necessary to jettison the canopy by use of a separate handle before ejection, and cases occurred in which the aircraft stopped spinning after the canopy was released. This led to proposals to use canopy jettison as a spin recovery technique; however, tests later showed that the reason why the aircraft stopped spinning in these circumstances was that removing the pilot's hand from the stick allowed the ailerons to centralise.

'Early in 1957 it was decided to carry out further spinning trials, using a Hunter 6 modified to the latest standard and fitted with comprehensive test instrumentation and recording equipment. The additional instrumentation assisted the pilot in understanding what was happening, whilst the recorders measured the many parameters which the pilot was unable to do himself, as well as providing evidence should the aircraft crash. An anti-spin parachute was stowed on the tail of the fuselage for use if normal recovery action was ineffective.

'Flt Lt Bobby Burns, the senior Hunter Project Officer, and Flt Lt Basil Dodd were selected to carry out the trials, and they made all the necessary preparations. Following trials by Hawkers, the aircraft [XE588] arrived during November 1957, and it was planned to start the trials without delay. However, at this stage the CO, Wg Cdr D.F. Dennis, decided to take the first flight himself [on 9 November]. The aircraft failed to recover from the initial spin, and he ejected, receiving serious injuries. Fortunately the flight recorder was recovered from the wreckage, and this showed that he had inadvertently held the aileron against the direction of spin.

'It took about four months to prepare a new aircraft, by which time the lead pilot had been posted, and I was allocated to work with Basil Dodd. Naturally I made careful preparations. The subsequent trial at Boscombe during March 1958 proved to be quite straightforward. But we always ensured we were well clear of cloud, and started from an altitude of 40,000ft, aiming to have recovered, or at least to have stopped spinning, by the time the aircraft was down to 20,000ft. The aircraft entered the spin readily from the straight or turning stall, with full rudder and the stick fully back, although a spin could also be induced by coarse use of the aileron alone at low speed. The spin was rather oscillatory and the rate of rotation was quite slow, but one had to remember that the rate of descent was about 20,000ft per minute, and that a considerable amount of height was lost in recovering from the ensuing dive. Normal recovery action of full opposite rudder followed by moving the stick fully forward was always effective, provided the ailerons were held neutral. If more than a quarter outspin aileron was applied as the stick went forward the spin characteristics changed completely. The nose dropped almost to the vertical, the yawing and buffeting disappeared and the rate of rotation increased dramatically, so that it felt as if the aircraft was in an aileron turn and not a spin. However, centralising the ailerons always resulted in recovery. Releasing the controls also produced a recovery, although this could take up to two turns, or more if outspin aileron had been applied. Fuel state and extension of flap or air brake seemed to have little effect on spin characteristics, and the aircraft did not

(cont.)

T.7 XL572 of 229 OCU (pictured at RAF Chivenor on 22 August 1971) was delivered to the OCU on 1 July 1958. On 27 August 1959 it took part in a spin demonstration with a CFS instructor and OCU instructor. The Hunter apparently failed to recover from the first spin and the CFS instructor, John Hardacre, ejected but was killed, while Dennis Yeardley, the OCU instructor, recovered from the spin and landed the aircraft safely. (*Laurie Reid*)

show any tendency towards entering an inverted spin from a normal entry or while in the spin. However, subsequent trials a few years later were to show that an inverted spin could be induced, given the right conditions.

'My conclusions from doing forty-four spins in the clean aircraft, plus a further twenty-three with underwing tanks, were that the Hunter characteristics were relatively innocuous, and that spin recovery was simple and reliable provided no outspin aileron was applied. These conclusions agreed with those of Basil Dodd, who had carried out a similar number of spins. When the two-seat Hunter came for trials a little later in 1958, I only did one trip, and my place was taken by Alan Merriman who had arrived on the squadron earlier that year.

'These trials vindicated our faith in the Hunter, and later the RAF decided that although squadron pilots would still be prohibited from spinning, the instructors of the Hunter OCU at Chivenor should be permitted to demonstrate spinning to trainees. However, they had first to be checked out in the Hunter T.7 by instructors from the Central Flying School (CFS). At this time I was still on 'A' Sqn, but as far as I know the two CFS instructors involved did not speak either to Boscombe Down or to Hawkers before going down to Chivenor. The net result was that on the first spin [on 27 August 1959] the aircraft [T.7 XL572] apparently failed to recover and the CFS instructor [John Hardacre] ejected, receiving fatal injuries in the process. Meanwhile, the OCU instructor [Dennis Yeardley] had problems in ejecting, and while he was struggling, the aircraft stopped spinning, so he brought it back to base. The subsequent Board of Inquiry believed it was possible that the aircraft had entered an inverted spin and recommended that inverted spinning trials be undertaken – these were carried out some time later and were a success. The outcome was that all practice Hunter spinning was still prohibited in the RAF. However, demonstrations of normal and inverted spinning in the Hunter were given by ETPS tutors to students, and other pilots who required the experience, for over forty years until the last Hunter T.7 was finally retired in August 2001.'

Flt Lt (later Sqn Ldr) Bernard Noble, 'A' Squadron, Boscombe Down, 1957–9

powered by the same Avon 113 as was fitted to the Hunter F.4, but the second prototype (XJ627), which was based on the F.6, and which first flew on 17 November 1956, was powered by the more powerful Avon 203. This engine was not adopted on production aircraft, however, a decision probably caused by the government cutbacks announced in 1957. At first the T.7, as the production model was known, was armed with two cannon in the nose but this was later reduced to just one gun with the deletion of the port Aden. Outwardly the T.7 differed from the fighter versions in having a longer nose, lengthened by 3ft. Some forty-five Hunter T.7s were built at Kingston, beginning in 1957, the first production model (XL563) flying on 11 October 1957. In 1958 Hunter T.7s entered RAF service with 229 OCU at Chivenor (from

January 1967 T.7s were also issued to 4 FTS at Valley, Anglesey, to supplement Gnat trainers in advanced pilot tuition). Later examples were issued to operational squadrons in RAF Fighter Command and 2nd Tactical Air Force (TAF) in Germany. During 1957 and 1958 six more Hunter T.7s were converted from F.4 airframes, and these were delivered between February and May 1959.

In May 1958 the first of forty-one Hunter T.8s, -B and -C dual-control trainers for the Royal Navy's carrier aircraft programme, was delivered to 764 Training Squadron at RNAS Lossiemouth. (The T.8 was not stressed for carrier operations and only ever operated from land bases.) F.4 WW664, which was converted to two-seat configuration, and with Mod.228 wings and arrestor hook, effectively became the prototype

F.6 XF375 of ETPS, based at Farnborough, flown by Flt Lt Graham Williams in 1966. During 1956–7 the Ministry of Supply and Armstrong Whitworth at Wymeswold and Bitteswell used this Hunter before it joined the English Electric Co. at Warton in January 1959. It joined the ETPS on 23 April 1963, moving to RAE in 1976. (*Richard Wilson*)

Opposite: In June 1962 T.8 XL580, seen here in 1976, became the 'Admiral's Barge' when it was allocated to 764 Squadron FOFT (Flag Officer Flying Training) at RNAS Yeovilton. Note the admiral's pennant painted on the nose and the white surround applied to the national insignia. XL580 first flew on 30 May 1958, and in June 1980 became one of three T.8s (the other two were XL602 and XL603) converted to T.8M by BAe to be used by 899 Squadron to acquaint Sea Harrier FRS.1 pilots under training with Ferranti Blue Fox radar equipment. (*HAL* via *Frank Mason*)

T.8M XL602 wearing the famous 'Bunch with the Punch' markings of No. 899 Squadron, Royal Navy, taxiing in. Note the AIM-9L Sidewinder missile simulator on the outboard wing pylon. (*Mick Jennings*)

T.8M XL602 of 899 Squadron (RN), one of three modified to house the Ferranti Blue Fox radar system fitted to the Sea Harrier FRS.1, over Dunsfold in August 1978. XL602 was built as a T.8 and was flown for the first time on 18 November 1958 by Duncan Simpson and delivered to 764 Squadron (RN) on 30 December that year. In August 1964 it joined 759 Squadron, being converted to T.8M by BAe at Brough in March 1980. (*BAe*)

T.8B WW664 of 764 Squadron (RN) at RNAS Lossiemouth on 19 July 1969, shortly before conversion to T.75 (514) for the Singaporean Air Force. Built at Blackpool as an F.4, WW664 was issued to 26 Squadron but it was damaged in a forced landing at Ahlhorn on 28 May 1956. The aircraft was returned to Dunsfold whereupon it was converted to two-seat configuration, with Mod.228 wings and arrestor hook, and came to be regarded as the prototype T.8. WW664 first flew in T.8 configuration on 3 March 1958 and early in May successfully completed brief trials at Boscombe Down. When a Navy requirement for operational training on the Tactical Air Navigation (TACAN) system was received in 1963, WW664 became the prototype for the T.8B with full TACAN equipment. (*Adrian Balch*)

T.8. It paved the way for the first-phase delivery of twenty-seven T.8s to the Navy. Ten were new-build T.8s diverted from the RAF T.7 contract, the first, XL580, being delivered on 1 May 1958 (it was lost during a low-level roll at Lossiemouth only five days later). A conversion order followed for eighteen F.4s (one of which was WW664) to be brought up to T.8 standard during 1958 and 1959. In 1963 a Navy requirement for operational training on the Tactical Air Navigation (TACAN) system led to the delivery of four T.8B aircraft with full TACAN equipment (WW664 now became the T.8B prototype, while the other three were converted F.4s). An order for ten F.4s to be converted to T.8C with partial TACAN equipment followed. T.8 XL604, which had been returned to Hawkers after being overstressed during aerobatics, was converted to T.8C standard and came to be regarded as the T.8C prototype. On 22 November 1963, following brief trials, XL604 joined 759 (Training) Squadron at RNAS

Brawdy, where it was followed by the arrival of ten further T.8C aircraft. The TACAN Hunters gave valuable and extensive service. Seven T.8s were lost in accidents. In June 1980 three were converted to T.8M to be used to acquaint Sea Harrier pilots under training with Blue Fox radar equipment.

'The most trouble-free aircraft I ever came across – from Swordfish to Scimitar.' So said Snr Artificer Jack Rowe BEM of 764 Naval Air Squadron, an air weapons training squadron based at Lossiemouth. Rowe was awarded his medal for fitting an AIM Sidewinder installation into a Hunter drop-tank in February 1962: 'Firing of Sidewinders in training was a very pricey business. After much thought I had a drop-tank converted to take the head of a Sidewinder, the remainder of the black boxes being housed within the tank. A note in the pilot's headset indicated a "hit". This installation saved huge sums!'

CHAPTER 3

HUNTER HEYDAY

The Hunter F.4 differed greatly from the F.1 and F.2. F.4s were powered by the Avon RA 7, rated 113 or 115, the latter modified to reduce engine surge. They had additional fuel capacity – courtesy of increased internal fuel cells and two 100-gallon drop-tanks on inboard wing pylons – as well as provision for underwing stores and a 'full flying tail'. Some 365 Hunter F.4s were built by Hawkers at Kingston and Blackpool, the first, WT701, flying on 20 October 1954 in the hands of Frank Murphy. WW646, the first Blackpool-built F.4, flew for the first time on 20 January 1955. In April Hunter F.4s began arriving at West Raynham for use with the Air Fighting

Development Squadron (AFDS) and DFLS. During the year F.4s re-equipped 247 and 54 Squadrons at Odiham, where they replaced Hunter F.1s, and 111 Squadron at North Weald, where they replaced Meteor F.8s. No. 229 OCU at Chivenor and the Flying College at Manby in Lincolnshire also took delivery of the F.4.

In 2nd TAF in Germany the Hunter F.4 replaced all ten squadrons of Sabre F.1/F.4s in the Brüggen, Geilenkirchen, Jever, Oldenburg and Wildenrath Wings, and the DH Venom FB.1 in 98, 118 and 14 Squadrons of the Fassberg Wing. In 1955 the Jever Wing became the first in Germany to receive the Hunter F.4. The 'Jever Steam Laundry' (as it was known) became a four

No. 26 Squadron F.6s of No. 124 Wing, 2nd TAF, on the pan at RAF Gütersloh, 1957. No. 26 Squadron, with their distinctive springbok markings, served at Oldenburg on Sabres then Hunter F.4s before disbanding in 1957 and reforming in 1958. (*Chris W. Cowper* via *Alan Pollock*)

Opposite, above: Flt Lt Bill Boult and Flg Off Ken Jones of No. 26 Squadron walk out to their Hunters at RAF Gütersloh, 1957. (via *Alan Pollock*)

'As for many others, 26 was my first squadron. My stay, mid-1953 to late '56, was one of great change from the post-Korean War rapid expansion to the Duncan Sandys "Missile Era" contraction. It was also a time of change in leadership, control and discipline from the "laissez-faire", high risk, gung-ho, train-busting attitude of the old 2nd TAF, with frequent funeral parades to the British Cemetery in Hamburg, to the more responsible and accountable conduct which followed the air exercise "Coronet" in 1953, when slaughter ensued throughout. A new phrase, "Rules of Engagement", was introduced and the number of funeral parades declined.

'In the winter of 1953 the Vampire gave way to the Sabre. This was like Grand Prix after go-carting. Whatever we were to fly in future years nothing would displace the Sabre as number one in our affection. Although underpowered, short on fuel and lightly armed, it was a superb flying machine, which inspired great confidence in all who had the good fortune to fly it. Later we learned, not surprisingly, that when the aircraft were returned to the Maintenance Unit (MU), on re-equipping with Hunters, airframe inspections revealed that the majority had cracked main spars. "Aircraft Fatigue" was introduced into our vocabulary and our Gs were limited as result. In my opinion, other than the weapon punch, the Hunter was never as satisfying to fly as the Sabre. Above all, it was battle-proven against the MiG.

'During a 124 Wing detachment to Cyprus in 1955 we learned we were to re-equip immediately with Hunters before our Squadron Standard presentation by the Duke of Edinburgh. On our arrival home the Hunter conversion was completed by A Flight, while B Flight continued with Sabre operations, including the Battle Flight commitment. This meant they were dispersed around the runway threshold with grandstand views of every Hunter landing. Their proximity had a significant effect on the conversion course. Even on our first flights, which should have consisted of general handling at height, then a couple of circuits before a final landing, we flew away to somewhere in the low-flying area to practise tight, power-off circuits. We then ran in to break and do the tightest circuit we dared. One of our pilots lost control close to touch-down and crashed through the runway caravan and crash vehicles, decapitating the unfortunate occupants.

'During the Hunter period 26 Squadron decided to form an aerobatic team. This been attempted with the slatted-wing Sabres but these had proved to be a little too temperamental in close formation and high Gs when various slats would be "inning" and "outing" caused an untidy unsteadiness. The hard edgers would have been different. Geoff Wilkinson, the squadron's most respected pilot, was the obvious leader and competition started for places. Being determined to get into the team and on the chance that no one else would choose to fly on the left wing, I volunteered to be No. 3. The team emerged as Geoff, Tony Funnell, Pete Perry and myself. Later it was decided to fly a reserve as No. 5 and Bob Chase took this role. We used to fly our practice sessions at the conclusion of the day's flying programmes. These became enjoyable, demanding and satisfying experiences, as we ran through our short routine. Geoff was a super leader with a firm, smooth, consistent style and a calm R/T commentary voice. We became the 2nd TAF representative team and the CO at the time, John Severne, commissioned a squadron painting.'

Mike Haggerty, 26 Squadron pilot, 2nd TAF, 1953–6

'On 26 April 1956, after a detachment to the French Air Force base at Luxeuil, the squadron received its first Hawker Hunter Mk 4, XF306, later to become "E", the pilots sat brooding over Pilots Notes and trying out the Hunter cockpit for size. It was smaller and more cramped than the Sabre cockpit but the pilots were pleased to have the Martin Baker ejection seat with the face blind, an improvement, it was considered, on the American "bang seat" which was operated from the arm rests. By the 10th the aircraft were being painted with the sharks-teeth, and the general opinion was that the Hunter looked better than the Sabre with the markings. Two major crises came to a head in October and November with the Suez invasion and the Russian repression of the Hungarian uprising. Both of these resulted in the Wing (112, 71, 67 and 130 Squadrons) being warned to be ready for war. The wives on the "married patch" were strongly advised to learn to drive, if they didn't know already, and be prepared to make their own way to the Channel ports. However, by Christmas, the panic had subsided.'

Flt Lt Robin A. Brown, 112 Squadron Hunter F.4 pilot, Shark Squadron: The History of 112 Squadron, 1917–1975, *Crecy, 1994*

Below: Pictured at Halton on 28 September 1985 is F.4 XF319, which was delivered to the RAF on 25 January 1956 and joined 112 'Shark' Squadron. Sqn Ldr Neville Duke was a 'Shark' pilot and he finished the war as the top-scoring RAF pilot in the Middle East Theatre. No. 112 Squadron received its first Hunter F.4 (XF306) on 26 April 1956. This and the other Hunter F.4s that replaced the Canadair Sabre F.4s soon received the customary 'sharks-teeth', though they were complicated to spray paint, and each one could take up to 48 hours to complete. At the suggestion of Flt Lt Robin Brown, the squadron commander's aircraft, XF319/A, was used to revive the wartime 'query symbol' on its fuselage. (*Adrian Balch*)

'I was posted to 20 Squadron in 1955 at RAF Oldenburg, 2nd TAF, as an engine mechanic. At that time the squadron was flying Sabre aircraft. That year, or early in 1956, we were re-equipped with Hunter Mk 4s, along with 26 Squadron, also at Oldenburg. I believe we were two of the first squadrons to receive this aircraft in 2nd TAF. We ground crew found it a dream to work on after the old Sabre. It was certainly a pilot's aircraft, not only because of what it could do in the air, but also its high serviceability rate. However, the pods, which collected ammunition clips when air-firing, tended to fall off in flight owing to the weak spring-loaded clips used for fastening. One four-aircraft detachment, to Aalborg in Denmark, had to return to Oldenburg because a Hunter lost its pods in flight. The detachment did take place, although several hours later than planned. A modification to the fastening clips overcame the problem. One could never trust the cartridge start system. They were awkward to fit and would not always fire first time. This always seemed to happen when the pilots wanted to get airborne quickly. Later, when the squadron had Mk 6s, this system had been replaced with an AVPIN* starter, a much more reliable starter system but messy and a dangerous fluid.

'The squadron had a visit from Hawker's chief test pilot Neville Duke, who spoke to the pilots about the in-flight re-ignition problems the aircraft was having at that time. Incidentally, he arrived in an Anson and not a flash Hunter, which we all expected.

'No. 20 Squadron had a tortoise as a mascot [which] used to do its flying in a cardboard box jammed in with the pilot. It had its own logbook, and on one occasion when all the squadron personnel had chest X-rays, I taped it to the screen for its own X-ray. It certainly had a number of "Hunter Hours".'

Flt Sgt Ken Bullard, 20 Squadron, 1955

*AVPIN, proper name isopropylnitrate, was a mono starter fuel, which created its own oxygen as it burned so it could be used in a totally enclosed ignition chamber. In its liquid state it had a distinctive sweet smell. Burnt, it had a distinct, sharp odour, shared only with other select AVPIN-started aircraft.

squadron Hunter wing operating in the dual role of air defence and ground attack. Nos 98 and 118 Squadrons began receiving F.4s in April 1955. In June, 14 Squadron re-equipped with the F.4 and moved to Oldenburg where 20 and 26 Squadrons converted from the Sabre F.1. At Jever in January 1956, 93 Squadron began replacing its Sabre F.1s with Hunter F.4s, and 4 Squadron began replacing its Sabre F.4s with Hunter F.4s early the same year. At Brüggen, in April and May 1956, 67, 71, 112 and 130 Squadrons gave up their Sabre F.1/F.4s for Hunter F.4s. Finally, in May and June 1956, 3 and 234 Squadrons at Geilenkirchen began their re-equipment with the Hunter F.4 replacing the Sabre F.1.

A conversion contract to modify thirty-three Hunter F.6 aircraft to FR.10 standard for the reconnaissance role had been received in 1958 to meet a need to replace the Supermarine Swift FR.5 in 2nd TAF in Germany and the Meteor FR.9 in the Far East. (In Aden FR.10s operated with 1417 Flight, of which more later.) The FR.10 differed principally from the F.6 in having three forward-looking reconnaissance cameras in the nose, where they replaced the radar-ranging scanner and camera gun. Armour plate had to be fitted under the cockpit floor as ballast. Though no provision was made for rocket armament and the DME (Distance Measuring Equipment) was deleted, the FR.10 retained the four Aden cannon and could therefore undertake a secondary air defence role if required. One of the problems with the Swift FR.5 was its lack of range, but with 230-gallon drop-tanks the FR.10 could fly from Germany to Malta non-stop if required. XF429, the first conversion, flew for the first time on 7 November 1958. No. 2 Squadron of 2nd TAF was the first to receive FR.10s in 1960, followed by 4 Squadron, where they replaced Hunter F.4s, both squadrons together forming RAF Germany's Tactical Reconnaissance Wing.

Opposite, below: FR.10 WW593 of 14 Squadron at RAF Gütersloh in October 1972. (*Adrian Balch*)

FR.10 XE585 of 4 (FR) Squadron at Gibraltar on 7 June 1968. Built at Kingston as an F.6, XE585 was first flown on 16 September 1956 by Hugh Merewether. It went on to serve with the CFE and the DFLS at West Raynham, before being returned to Hawkers on 16 September 1959 for conversion to FR.10 standard. In March 1971 XE585 was purchased by Hawkers and converted again, this time to T.66E (S.1392) for delivery to the Indian Air Force in December 1973. (*Adrian Balch*)

No. 4 Squadron returned to England in 1970 to convert to the Harrier. In December 1970, 2 Squadron began conversion to the Phantom FGR.2 at Brüggen, operating its last FR.10s from Gütersloh in February 1971. The FR.10 enjoyed a long association with 2nd TAF, but the Hunter F.4, in contrast, enjoyed only a short career with the majority of squadrons in Germany.

In addition to the Hawker-built F.4s, by August 1955 a total of 105 Sapphire-powered F.5s were produced by Armstrong Whitworth at Baginton. This version, created by introducing similar fuel system modifications to those of the Hunter F.4, first flew on 19 October 1954. In March 1955, 263 Squadron at Wattisham began replacing its Sapphire-engined F.2s with F.5s and in May they replaced the Swifts operated by 56 Squadron at Waterbeach, Cambridgeshire. A month later Hunter F.5s replaced the Meteor F8s of 41 Squadron at Biggin Hill and those of 1 Squadron at Tangmere. In July 257 Squadron received Hunter F.5s to replace its existing Hunter F.2s. In November 222 Squadron at Leuchars received F.4s in August. In December, 34 Squadron at Tangmere began re-equipping with the F.5.

In the UK 43 Squadron at Leuchars replaced its Hunter F.1s with F.4s in February–March 1956. In March–April 92 and 66 Squadrons at Linton-on-Ouse gave up their Sabre F.4s and also re-equipped with the Hunter F.4. Thirteen fighter squadrons

> 'I spent 3½ years on 56 Squadron, which was equipped with Sapphire-engined Hunter Mk 5 aircraft in 1955 following the demise of the Swifts Mk 1 and 2. Reliability of the Mk 5 suffered badly in the first year or so, mainly due to the engine fuel control components. However, reliability rocketed with disbandment of 63 Squadron and some of the Avon-engined Mk 6 aircraft were used to re-equip 56 Squadron.'
> *Cpl Dave Stint, engine fitter, 56 Squadron, RAF Waterbeach, January 1954–September 1959*

were now equipped with the Hunter F.4 in 2nd TAF and seven more in the UK. In October 1956 Hunter F.5s of 1 and 34 Squadrons flew from Tangmere to Cyprus to be in position to provide top cover over Egypt for British and French aircraft involved in Operation Musketeer, the Anglo-French occupation of the Suez Canal zone in Egypt. On 2 November the Hunters, carrying the yellow and black Suez identification stripes, flew a number of top cover sorties in support of naval fighter-bombers. However, their limited endurance permitted the Hunters only a short time over the patrol area. This, together with the Egyptian Air Force's almost total absence, resulted in the Hunters being operated as base defence at Akrotiri and Nicosia to deter possible incursions over Cyprus by Egyptian Il-28 bombers. No air-to-air encounters were reported and 1 and 34 Squadrons returned to Tangmere. No. 1 Squadron was the last to operate the F.5, disbanding at Tangmere on 23 June 1958. No. 263 Squadron at Stradishall disbanded a week later but was immediately re-numbered 1 Squadron.

No. 74 'Tiger' Squadron at Horsham St Faith near Norwich received Hunter F.4s in March 1957 and operated these until F.6s began arriving during November 1957–January 1958. (In April 1957, 245 Squadron at Stradishall became the last to receive F.4s but had them for only two months before the squadron was disbanded on 30 June.) Flg Off Ian Cadwallader, a New Zealander in 'Tiger' Squadron, was one of the original Hunter pilots on 74 Squadron. He had transferred to the RAF in 1954 while training on Harvards in the RNZAF, part of a Commonwealth scheme to keep a few New Zealanders in the RAF. Two others from the same course were the first Kiwis under the scheme to get their 'wings' since the war, at Middleton St George, at 4 FTS:

I first flew the Hunter at OCU at Chivenor and I managed to get a T.7 up to 53,000ft. Mind you, it

Tiger, Tiger

'All our second-hand Hunters made funny noises! We did not really know what they were and we did not realize that they were signs of age and wear and should not have been there at all. WV269 made such noises. I was in a battle pair with Tony Dean over Cambridge at 35,000ft when there was an enormous bang and the aircraft started to vibrate. Almost instinctively I shut the engine down, which stopped all the bangs and thumps. Full of the confidence of youth, I decided to take the aircraft home. Everything was fine until I turned on to finals at Horsham and found I was too high. I applied full aileron and full opposite rudder, whereupon the aircraft almost rolled over on to its back (at which point those watching on the airfield below doffed their caps!), but it had the desired effect and I lost height quite dramatically! I put it down on the runway rather fast at about 180 knots but the brakes worked well and I stopped the Hunter before the runway's end and turned off on to the ORP, relieved and pleased at getting down safely. But, instead of congratulations, I was told off for not inserting the pin in the ejection seat when I left the aircraft!'

Flg Off (later AVM) Boz Robinson, 74 Squadron, 1957

Boz was subsequently awarded a Green Endorsement. WV269, which first flew on 12 May 1955 and had previously been allocated to 54 Squadron, was re-engined and was soon flying again. It was eventually scrapped at Kemble in about 1961.

On 10 May 1957 eight 74 'Tiger' Squadron Hunters left Horsham for Chièvres on an exchange with the Belgian Air Force, but before they left a photo opportunity was created by the presence in Norwich of Bertram Mills' Circus, as Ian Cadwallader recalls: 'We persuaded Mr Alex Kerr, the trainer, to bring his tiger Begum to Horsham for a photo session.' Begum was photographed with pilots and their Hunters. There were certainly some reservations about this event, but on the day both tiger and pilots behaved well! Sqn Ldr Keith Haselwood, the CO, was told by Alex to give Begum a sharp rap over the ears with a whip if she misbehaved! The Boss was understandably relieved that he had no need to resort to such measures, and in retrospect the resultant pictures were considered to be well worth the bravado! Putting the tiger's head on the aircraft was a project given to Ian Cadwallader when 74 Squadron got Hunters: 'A suitable design to put between the yellow and black bars had to be found because the small tiger's head we had on the engine cowl on the Meteor looked like a pussycat! So after establishing the size, I cut two stencils, one just the shape, which we sprayed yellow, and the other had the cut-outs for the black bits. The boys in the hangar did the spraying, then I did all the touching up of the other colours with a small brush. The whiskers had to be about 1cm wide so that they could be seen. A tiger without whiskers looks ridiculous! Our Christmas card that year had a photo of Tony Hilton in the cockpit with the tiger reaching up towards him.' Begum was adopted as the squadron mascot, and at the end of 1958 the 'Tigers' were invited to Olympia to see Begum perform. Sadly, she was to die a few weeks later. (*Ian Cadwallader*)

wasn't flying very well at that altitude but when I rolled over and pulled through it went downhill very well, going supersonic very quickly. It was virtually impossible to read the altimeter, so discretion being the better part of valour, I didn't need to be told that it was time to pull this aeroplane back into level flight, which I achieved at about 12,000ft. At the age of 20 it sure beat the hell out of fast cars! After OCU I was posted, in April 1956, to 74 Squadron on Meteor 8s and thoroughly enjoyed flying them for about nine months until we got Hunters, which I flew for nearly two years. The Hunter was not only the best looking fighter of its time but it was a magnificent aeroplane to fly and I consider myself extremely fortunate to have been in the right place at the right time to be posted to the right squadron! In my time at Horsham St Faith it was quite a fantastic life for young men. There were about twenty pilots on the squadron and most of us were single, under twenty-five, and we lived in the luxury of a very comfortable Officers' Mess. We all had a batman, so we never had to iron a shirt or clean our shoes or make our bed. The hours we worked, other than when on an exercise, were not arduous, and we always flew in pairs, so we learned to trust and depend on each other and we loved doing what we did. In our leisure time we usually stuck together and a fair bit of partying went on. The only pilots who didn't live in the mess were those who were married and we used to think of them as the older guys. I well remember when a new Flt Lt was due to be posted in as a flight commander and the boss told us he was thirty years old. Someone said, 'Hell, a geriatric!'

EXERCISE VIGILANT

During Exercise Vigilant, which took place on 25–7 May 1957, 450 raiding aircraft, V-bombers included, were ranged against the defences of Fighter Command. The Hunters of 74 'Tiger' Squadron at Horsham St Faith achieved a high interception rate during the exercise and they were particularly pleased with a turnaround time of 12 minutes for each aircraft under the stringent conditions imposed. Normal practice was for two aircraft to be constantly on standby to scramble or to replace those aircraft already in the air and whose fuel was getting low. Based squadrons would take turns at filling this very short notice alert. At dawn on the first day, Flg Offs Boz Robinson and Tony Hilton were scrambled. LAC Ken Hazell, a squadron armourer, tells what happened next:

The flight lines at St Faith were busy with ground crew getting aircraft ready for the day's flying. My squadron had eight Hunter F.4s, the fins of which we whitewashed so that other aircraft knew which side they were on. Also operating from St Faith while Coltishall's runway was being extended were the two Coltishall Javelin FAW.4 squadrons, Nos 23 and 141. When the order came to 'scramble', our eight Hunters began taking off, followed by the Javelins. We then saw the fire trucks race towards the end of the runway and we were informed that Hunter 'H for Hotel' [WV269/H] had failed to get airborne during take off because of a control fault which put it into manual reversion. The pilot, Flt Lt Tony Davies, was unhurt.

Davies had overshot the runway, smashed through the fence on the edge of the airfield, skimmed across the main road running alongside

White-finned F.6s of 65 Squadron from Duxford lined up at Horsham St Faith on 25 May 1957 for the first day of Exercise Vigilant. In the background are 23 Squadron's Javelins. The white fins were to identify 'home'-based Hunters. XE593/P, the nearest aircraft, was destroyed in a starter explosion at Duxford on 23 January 1961. (*Ian Cadwallader*)

The almost unrecognizable forward fuselage of Flg Off Tony Hilton's F.6 XE662 'S for Sugar' which crashed at Horsham St Faith on 25 May 1957, the first day of Exercise Vigilant. Hilton ejected safely but his right elbow was broken in fourteen places when the ejection seat hit the runway, trapping his arm. (*Ian Cadwallader*)

Pilots of 74 'Tiger' Squadron inspecting the wreckage of XE662. (*Ian Cadwallader*)

its western boundary and pancaked in a ploughed field opposite with the aircraft tail overhanging the grass verge. Fortunately there was no traffic at the time. WV269/H was later towed back to the hangar with slight damage.

Hazell continues:

A Javelin FAW.4 [XA732] then left the 23 Squadron line and began taxiing towards our line. We noticed that one of the underbody ventral fuel tanks had dropped down at one end and was scraping on the tarmac, causing sparks, which quickly turned into flame. Several of us grabbed CO_2 fire extinguishers (the fire tenders had already gone to the aid of Flt Lt Davies) and ran to the taxiway to alert the two-man crew. They looked at us but continued to taxi towards the control tower.

The Javelin's large delta wing meant the tank failure was hidden from the crew and the pilot taxied on, unaware of the problem, pushing the nose of the 'bosom' tank along the ground, the noise unnoticed because of the scream of the engines. The Javelin continued to taxi, trailing flame and black smoke. Air Traffic's urgent call – 'You are on fire!' – was obviously directed at the Javelin crew, but it was heard by Flg Off Hilton, pilot of Hunter XE662 'S for Sugar', with disastrous results. Hazell again:

Suddenly, from nowhere, we saw this Hunter skidding along the grass doing what looked like a wheels-up landing. 'S for Sugar' hit the runway cross section and the nose section broke away from the main fuselage where the gun-pack was fitted. The pilot was thrown out in his ejection seat and he lay on the ground injured.

Hilton had heard Air Traffic's 'on fire' message to the Javelin and thought the message was directed at him, so he had decided to get down as quickly as he could! Turning in short, he blew the wheels down and without ceremony force-landed across the airfield, putting the Hunter down hard. It bounced and broke up, the impact fracturing the fuselage behind the cockpit and simultaneously firing the

primary charge of the ejection seat. The aircraft continued to slide along the ground, the wing slicing through a tent, and went on to demolish several bicycles. Hilton's parachute had deployed meanwhile and he floated back to earth, landing in front of the bemused ambulance and fire crews who were rushing to the assistance of Tony Davies.

Ian Cadwallader takes up the story.

I watched Tony turn in short and try to put the aircraft down with the gear only half down. It was sickening watching the aircraft bounce two or three times and then the front section broke off and the seat fired. Meantime the Javelin burned merrily on! Tony came down still in the seat and landing with his elbow between the taxiway and the seat shattered his elbow.

Hilton's elbow was badly damaged and never regained full movement, although he was able to return to flying. Ken Hazell concludes:

Meanwhile, the Javelin was well ablaze and stopped at the hardstanding being used by 141 Squadron's Javelins where it burnt out, leaving half a wing and the jet-pipes. At this stage St Faith was stood down from the Exercise.

'When I returned to St Faith there was the most extraordinary sight of smoke, wreckage and devastation. There were still a lot of us in the air in our exercise-marked, white-finned Hunters. We had all found plenty of targets and had pushed our fuel to the absolute limits. Coltishall was out of action: its runways were being resurfaced and we could get nothing out of a shell-shocked ATC at St Faith so we went to West Raynham, praying that our fuel would last, but found that here Air Traffic were totally preoccupied with something like sixteen aircraft waiting to land. The fuel situation demanded that we find a suitable gap among the Meteors, Meteor night-fighters, Javelins and Hunters and get down. Having landed, it was literally a case of steering among aircraft that had rolled to a halt out of fuel.'
Flg Off (later AVM) Boz Robinson, 74 Squadron,
Exercise Vigilant, 25 May 1957

F.6 XE662 'S for Sugar', which ended up in a tented area at Horsham St Faith. Astonishingly, no one was killed in the accident. (*Ian Cadwallader*)

Plans, begun as far back as 1952, to produce a supersonic Hunter (P.1083), using an afterburning RA 14 Avon engine and 50-degree swept-wing, had been finally dashed on 13 July 1953 with the cancellation of the prototype, coinciding as it did with the ending of the Korean War. If the change in wing sweep had gone ahead, the P.1083 might well have achieved supersonic performance in level flight, but without the change the Hunter was destined to operate at subsonic speeds whatever the engine. On 17 November 1951 Rolls-Royce had bench-run the RA 14 engine, which by April 1952 was producing an output of 10,500lb static thrust. This engine was chosen to power the next Hunter variant, the F.6. Though designated as an interceptor, Hawkers really developed the F.6 with the ground attack role in mind. Having successfully replaced the 100 gallon drop-tanks on the Hunter F.4 with 1,000lb bombs, Hawkers had identified the feasibility of mounting

'My first Hunter solo was at Chivenor (the OCU) in May 1958. The problem was coming to terms with powered flying controls. During the first few minutes of the sortie I flew around with slight wing waggling as you tended to over control until you got used to the very light powered controls. In those days there was very little "feel". (The Lightning, of course, had fully powered controls but it also had excellent artificial "feel".) I also remember the first time I went supersonic. The Hunter, of course, required a fairly steep dive and you only reached about Mach 1.05. (Unlike the Lightning, which was more than able to go supersonic in a big way while in a fairly steep climb!) I arrived at Horsham St Faith to join 74 Squadron in August 1958. It had already been re-equipped with the Hunter F.6 which was considerably more powerful than the F.4 (which I had flown at Chivenor). It was even more fun. The spirit and morale on 74 – The Tigers – was extraordinary. And visits to the Trowel & Hammer and other Norwich and Broadland pubs were an almost nightly experience. Young pilots were shown the way by the likes of Boz Robinson – both in the air and round the pubs! There was a lot of high-level battle formation, which kept young pilots like me very busy. One thing I shall always remember is doing aerobatics in the Hunter. It was so exhilarating and yet so relaxing! A good session of aeros and you felt years younger!'

David Jones, Hunter F.6 pilot, 74 'Tiger' Squadron, Horsham St Faith, 1958

F.6s of 66 Squadron at RAF Acklington, Northumberland, late August 1958. XE618/ES is probably a replacement for XG233, which crashed into Famagusta Bay on 20 August during the Squadron's detachment to Cyprus. The pilot was flying low over the sea in poor visibility, haze and sun when he hit the sea with fatal results. XE618, which first flew on 12 June 1956, was converted to FGA.9, being delivered to 208 Squadron on 4 February 1960. After serving also with 8 Squadron, in December 1967 XE618 joined the Kuwaiti Air Force. XK139/G first flew on 21 March 1957 and was delivered to the RAF on 12 August. It was converted to FGA.9, being delivered to 1 Squadron on 19 September 1961. (*Alastair Aked*)

four rocket tiers under each outer wing so that up to twenty-four 3-inch rocket projectiles could be carried in addition to the inboard bombs or drop-tanks. Meanwhile, at English Electric the P.1 was developed (as the Lightning) to properly fulfill the role of the RAF's first true supersonic front-line interceptor.

The Hunter F.6 evolved from the P.1099, which was created by marrying uprated production wings equipped with four pylon hardpoints to the redundant P.1083 fuselage and installing the Rolls-Royce Avon RA 14 engine. Neville Duke flew the P.1099 prototype (XF833) from Dunsfold on 23 January 1954 but subsequent problems with the new engine resulted in changes, and it was derated to 10,000lb static thrust and became

the Avon 203. P.1099 flight trials were resumed on 20 July 1954 and the test programme ended successfully. Seven F.1 airframes were quickly converted to 'interim Mk 6' standard to serve as pre-production aircraft, the first, WW592, being flown by Bill Bedford on 25 March 1955. Unfortunately, no one, not even the designers at Hawkers, thought for a moment that redundant F.4 airframes could be adapted to accommodate the bigger, more powerful engine. It was only after the scrapping of numerous F.4 and F.5 airframes during the period 1960–3 that the attitude changed. It was cost-effective to rebuild Hunter F.4s to take the Avon 200-series engine after all.

By mid-1956 just over a hundred F.6s had been built. Early production models were fitted with a

No. 74 Squadron's Hunter F.6s (Flg Off J.A. Dean's F.6 XE591/G nearest) and Gloster Javelin FAW.4s of 23 Squadron on an operational turnaround at Horsham St Faith in 1957. The Javelin FAW.4s of 23 and 141 Squadrons, which were relocated from Coltishall during October 1956–May 1959 while the runway was resurfaced, formed the first Javelin Wing in Fighter Command while detached to Horsham. (*Ian Cadwallader*)

Flg Off Clive Wallis taxies past during a turnaround at Horsham St Faith in 1957. Note the smoke stains around the gun port. This F.6 was taking part in what was called an operational turnaround: this involved eight Hunters going off together with all cannon loaded, climbing to 40,000ft and firing off all ammunition before returning to base. All the aircraft would then be reloaded and go up to do the same again. The whole exercise was timed and reports sent to Fighter Command HQ. (*Ian Cadwallader*)

Flg Off J.A. Dean's F.6 XE591/G being re-armed during the operational turnaround. This Hunter served later with 65 Squadron and 229 OCU before being repurchased by Hawker Siddeley Aircraft on 4 April 1966 for conversion to Saudi Arabian Hunter F.60 (60/602), being delivered on 2 May 1966. (*Ian Cadwallader*)

Hunters of 92 Squadron lined up on the aircraft servicing platform (ASP) at Hal Far, Malta, on 9 January 1958 before departing to Nicosia in Cyprus for Armament Practice Camp (APC). Sqn Ldr Mike Hobson's F.6 XG239/MH was lost a few days later, on 11 January, when it crashed on take-off from Nicosia. The pilot survived and the aircraft was struck off charge. Behind is XG225/M, which first flew on 20 October 1956 and served with 20 and 74 Squadrons before joining 92 Squadron. (*Mike Hobson*)

variable-incidence tailplane, just as on previous marks, but all subsequent F.6 models had a 'flying tail' and extended-chord dogtooth wing. The Hunter F.6 was really a new aircraft and experienced Hunter pilots noticed the difference immediately. In October 1956 the first Hunter F.6s reached 19 Squadron at Church Fenton, Yorkshire, where they replaced Meteor F.8s, and in November they re-equipped 63 Squadron at Waterbeach. (This squadron was disbanded at Waterbeach in October 1958.) The next batch went to 111 Squadron at North Weald and 43 Squadron at Leuchars, where they replaced Hunter F.4s. In 1957 Hunter F.6s were issued to seven more squadrons: nos 54 and 247 at Odiham, 65 at Duxford, 66 at Acklington, 74 at Horsham St Faith, 263 at Stradishall and 92 at Middleton St George.

Sqn Ldr Mike Hobson assumed command of 92 Squadron on 8 April 1957. He recalls:

My tour was only 18 months, as I had just commanded 603 (City of Edinburgh) Squadron RAuxAF for a year at RAF Turnhouse until their disbandment in March 1957, and the meanies counted the two tours as one. I was appointed to 92 Squadron personally by the AOC, AVM Walter Cheshire (a renowned and feared disciplinarian), as 603 Squadron had been in the same Group, so he

knew me quite well. My conversion to the Hunter was a little unusual. As I had never flown a Hunter, nor indeed, any swept-wing aircraft, I contacted the 'Trainers' at Group HQ to ask for a conversion course at the OCU. This request was met with much hilarity and I was told that the courses were full for months to come, largely with foreign students. They asked me if I knew anyone on Hunters who would let me 'have a go'. I knew Ken Richardson, a flight commander on 222 Squadron at RAF Leuchars, so I rang him, to discover that the squadron was in Malta but that he was remaining behind with four aircraft to train some new pilots to operational standard.

Although he could ill afford the extra flying hours, Ken very kindly said he would see what he could do. Consequently, after a quick quiz on Pilots' Notes, given in the bar one evening by a bearded naval exchange officer, I launched off the next morning, 20 February 1957, into the wide blue yonder in a Hunter 4. (There were no dual aircraft or simulators.) I managed to do two sorties that day, two the following day and three on the third day, so eventually it was with the grand total of four hours and five minutes on type that I took over my squadron! Such a procedure seems almost unbelievable these days.

Although based at Middleton St George, 92 Squadron spent a great deal of time away from base on detachments (causing the inevitable marital problems, particularly among the airmen). There were NATO exercises when we deployed to the continent to bases such as Jever and Skrydstrup. I well remember the latter, for the Danes filled us up

F.6s N and XE532/L of 92 Squadron on the aircraft servicing platform at Nicosia, Cyprus, in January 1958 during the squadron's APC. XF520/K and XF522/D are in the tented hangars, right. In the background is the Kyrenia range. XE532/L first flew on 10 January 1956 and that same year was used for trials with various Avon engines and in tropical trials before joining 92 Squadron. XF522 was painted blue overall and became one of the mounts of the Blue Diamonds. It was struck off charge early in 1963. (*Mike Hobson*)

with contaminated fuel and we had two engine failures on take-off, both aircraft, fortunately, being brought to a stop before the overshoot.

We flew to Nicosia for our Armament Practice Camp on 9 January 1958, returning on 21 March. I made myself a little unpopular with the engineering staff in Malta on both occasions. We were due to stage through Luqa on the way out, but when I received the actual weather state while about 100 miles away, I decided that the crosswind was too strong for safety. The Hunter was not happy in a strong crosswind landing when carrying underwing fuel tanks, as we were. So I elected to land at Hal Far, which had a shorter runway, but into wind. Hal Far was a naval station with no Hunter equipment, so all the starting and servicing equipment, as well as the personnel, had to be loaded on to vehicles and trundled there from Luqa. This, of course, was not popular.

On the way home, three months later, a similar weather 'actual' was given to me so again I elected to land the squadron at Hal Far, among many mutterings once more from the engineering staff! Still, I got the squadron there and back with no mishaps! We had a very happy time at Nicosia and the permanent staff were very good to us and tolerant of the usual squadron high spirits, especially at Guest Nights. The AOC Cyprus during our stay was the delightful AVM W.J. 'Paddy' Crisham. He welcomed us to the island and laid on anything that we wanted. He was a Roman Catholic and his family was of such a size that the Works Department had to knock two quarters into one for his accommodation!

From 4 October 1957 to 1 October 1958, 92 Squadron operated from RAF Thornaby while the runway at Middleton St George was being resurfaced. The airfield had to be reactivated and some trees cut down at the end of the runway, which was only 1,800 yards long instead of our usual 2,000 yards. Group HQ thought that this could be a flight safety hazard, but during the whole of our operations from Thornaby we did not have one single incident due to landing or take-off. I think that the knowledge of the short runway concentrated our minds wonderfully on the approach, ensuring that we always touched down at exactly the right spot and at exactly the right speed! There was one amusing incident (in retrospect) at Thornaby. We were on a full flying programme, with Hunters taking off and landing every few minutes, and I happened to be in ATC when one of the controllers let out an astonished cry and pointed out a Morris Minor that had just turned on to the runway and was happily proceeding along it. Holding off all aircraft, I dispatched the fire tender to intercept the car and escort it back to the Control Tower, bringing the driver up to see me. Much to my amazement two gentlemen wearing clerical collars were ushered into the room, and on my asking them what on earth they thought they were doing, they informed me that they were going to the races at Redcar and that they 'always went this way!'

My tour on 92 Squadron finished on 15 October 1958 when I handed over to Sqn Ldr Bob Dixon. During the whole of my tour as squadron commander we did not have a single serious accident on the Hunter, but I lost Flg Off Ron Higgs in Cyprus when he was flying as passenger in a Sycamore. The tail rotor struck some trees on Mount Troodos and all aboard were killed.

A pair of 92 Squadron F.6s (left is XE532/L) at stand-by on a Sunday morning in February 1958 at Nicosia, Cyprus. (*Mike Hobson*)

Flt Lt Bill Kelly DFC, C Flight Commander in charge of the servicing team in 92 Squadron, photographed at Nicosia during the APC in February 1958. A 'father figure' on the squadron, 'Big' Bill Kelly was a large Canadian who celebrated his 35th birthday in Cyprus. He made his name at a squadron christening when he tossed the baby up in the air – and threw him right through a chandelier. Fortunately the baby suffered no ill effects, though he demolished the chandelier! (*Mike Hobson*)

222 Squadron's F.4s lined up at Leuchars, summer 1957. The nearest aircraft is WT771/C (note the chequers, which were raised to reduce the effects of exhaust burning), while behind is WV327/U. 222 Squadron disbanded after Exercise 'Strikeback' at the end of September 1957 as part of defence cuts. (*Grp Capt Ed Durham*)

Flt Lt John Howe of 'C' Flight, 222 Squadron, in front of F.4 WV327/U at Leuchars, summer 1957. In February 1960 Sqn Ldr John Howe (later AVM John Howe CB, CBE, AFC) took command of 74 'Tiger' Squadron at RAF Coltishall when it became the first RAF squadron to introduce the Lightning into service. (*Grp Capt Ed Durham*)

F.4 WV406/F of 222 Squadron with the Leuchars Officers Mess in the background, summer 1957. This Hunter first flew on 9 September 1955 and served later with No. 229 OCU at Chivenor and No. 3 CAACU at Exeter. (*Grp Capt Ed Durham*)

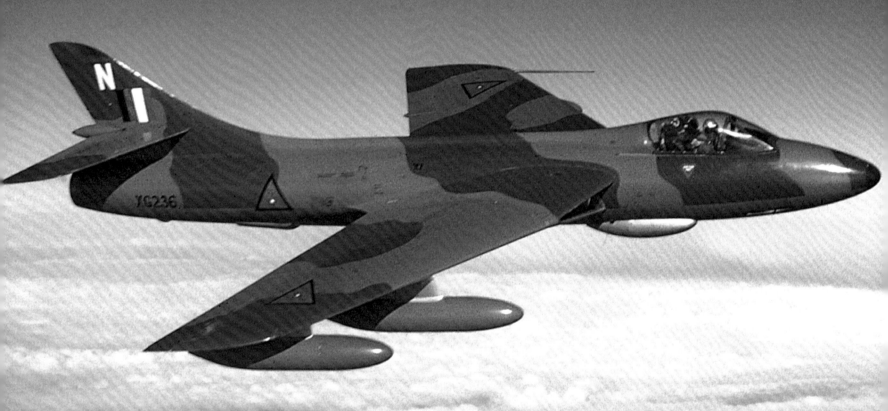

F.6 XG236/N photographed from XG251. Both these aircraft belonged to 66 Squadron, but had had their RAF roundels and fin flashes replaced by Iraqi triangular wing and pre-revolutionary fin flash markings, as they were en route to Iraq on 7 May 1957 to act as reserve aircraft for a flypast in Baghdad. XG236 and XG251 were both Kingston-built F.6s, XG236 being flown for the first time on 19 October 1956 by Duncan Simpson. It was delivered to the RAF on 9 November 1956 and issued to 66 Squadron from 5 MU. It was lost in a crash near the Scottish border on 14 February 1958 and the pilot was killed. XG251 had first flown on 20 October 1956 when David Lockspeiser had taken it aloft. Delivered to 5 MU on 26 November that year, it served with 66 Squadron before being returned to Hawker Siddeley Aircraft in about 1960 for conversion to FGA.9 standard. On 30 October 1969 HAS bought the aircraft and converted it to FGA.74 for the Singaporean Air Force. It was delivered on 10 December 1970. (*Alastair Aked*)

'In May 1957 66 Squadron was on detachment to Akrotiri, Cyprus, from Linton-on-Ouse, Yorkshire, with brand new Hunter Mk 6s, at that time one of the best fighters in the Mediterranean. We had flown out via Orange in France, Luqa in Malta, and El Adem in Libya – all easy sectors with two 100-gallon drop-tanks. In the early post-Suez era we had settled down in the Eastern Mediterranean, supported by 6 Squadron's Venoms based at Akrotiri, and more Hunters of 54 Squadron from Odiham as well as the United States 6th Fleet with Crusaders and the Royal Navy with Seahawks. In the absence of a threat from Nasser we practised intercepting NATO aircraft. It was always a challenge to tangle with a Crusader, whose rate of turn was poor in comparison with the Hunter. Trouble was that just as one got him into one's sights, he would turn on his afterburner and draw away at high speed. Sonic booming the carriers followed by a low pass was always fun, until one day I noticed that all the carrier's guns followed me. They were off to make a landing in Lebanon and were at action stations. (I remember attaining 55,000ft over Beirut when operating from Akrotiri. I reduced power to zero thrust and attempted to glide back to Cyprus, not quite making it by about 20 miles. The Hunter was a joy to fly in the clear skies of the Mediterranean.)

'After a while we did other things and found that there was a shortage of second pilots on 70 Squadron who flew Hastings. As a result we were welcome to assist them on their regular schedules to Aden, and at the same time find out how the other half lived at 200mph. The shopping in Aden was first class but we all swore that we would never become transport pilots. (Little did we know that the majority of us would end our flying days in Transport Command in the not-too-distant future. I was the oldest pilot on the squadron in 1957 at the age of 32, so the writing was on the wall. I moved on to Beverleys the following year, a move from the most beautiful aircraft the RAF ever operated to perhaps the ugliest, although with a heart of gold.)

'The ill-fated King Faisal II was still on the throne in Iraq at that time, and with the RAF's biggest base at Habbaniyah, the British were staunch allies. The USA had funded the purchase of Hunters for the RIAF and after initial training it was decided to have a flypast of all the new aircraft to impress senior politicians and ambassadors in Baghdad. To impress everyone it was deemed that 100 per cent serviceability was essential for the flypast, so the AOC Cyprus decided to send two 66 Squadron Hunters as reserve aircraft with their RAF roundels overpainted with the unique Iraqi triangle. Ned Kelly and myself were lucky enough to be chosen as pilots. With four 100-gallon drop-tanks fitted we departed for Iraq on 7 May. The flight time was two hours without navigation aids. In clear weather the Mk I Eyeball took us over Turkey and Kurdistan until we found the Tigris which flowed down to Baghdad. Our instructions were to avoid Syria, which was allied to Egypt and had shot down RAF aircraft in its airspace not that long before. The aircraft chosen were XG236 and XG521.

'This was to be my first visit to the Arab world and I was most impressed by the hospitality and friendship of the people I met. Two amusing disappointments stick in my mind. When we visited the Officers' Club they were playing Bingo and the first officer to shout "House" was dressed in traditional Arab dress. The officers of the Hunter squadron invited us out to a nightclub in Baghdad and we had preconceived ideas of naughty Middle Eastern establishments. It was quite the opposite; being a very smooth club and the entertainment would have done justice to the BBC. And of course our hosts could not have been more hospitable. Sadly, one of the pilots was executed a couple of years later for rocketing a barracks at Mosul. The CO of the Hunter squadron went on to become a senior officer in the Air Force and was assassinated in Cairo after being seen off at Baghdad by Saddam Hussein.'

Flt Lt Alastair Aked, Hunter pilot, 66 Squadron, Cyprus, 1957

F.6 XG253/A of 66 Squadron over Mount Olympus, Cyprus, in 1957. This aircraft was flown for the first time on 1 November 1956 by David Lockspeiser and was delivered to the RAF on 27 November 1956. Later converted to FGA.9 standard, it also served with 54 and 79 Squadrons as well as with 229 OCU. (*Alastair Aked*)

Close-up view of F.6 XG253/A of 66 Squadron over Cyprus in 1957. Akrotiri is to the right. (*Alastair Aked*)

Another view of F.6 XG236/N of 66 Squadron en route to Baghdad on 7 May 1957. (*Alastair Aked*)

The hand-over ceremony at Habbaniyah, Iraq, in May 1957 when five F.6 Hunters (XJ677/778/679/681/682), paid for from US funds, were presented officially to King Faisal II. Iraq received ten more F.6s – again paid for by American aid – in December 1957. Iraq's first Hunter squadron became operational at Habbaniyah in the spring of 1958, its pilots having been trained at 229 OCU Chivenor. The revolution which swept Saddam Hussein to power brought further deliveries of aircraft and spares to a temporary halt. It was not until early in 1963 that Iraq was allowed to purchase more aircraft, twenty-four ex-Belgian Air Force Hunters being refurbished to FGA.9 standard and delivered as Mk 59s and 59Bs. These were followed by a further twenty-three Hunters in 1965 and 1966. (*Alastair Aked*)

In 1957 Duncan Sandys' infamous Defence White Paper, influenced no doubt by Whitehall mandarins and various service chiefs with 'scrambled egg' on their caps, predicted that the ICBM would shortly render manned interceptor aircraft obsolete. They must all have ended up with egg on their faces because the effect on Britain's aviation industry was catastrophic. Hunter squadrons (especially in Germany) disappeared as fast as Britain's once-proud rail network did under Dr Beeching in the early 1960s. The government reduced the number of Hunter F.6s for the RAF by 100 aircraft, the fifth production contract for 153 F.6s being terminated after only 53 had been built, and a 1955 order for 50 F.6s was cancelled. All of the DH Venom squadrons and nine of the thirteen Hunter F.4 squadrons in 2nd TAF were disbanded almost immediately. All four squadrons of the Brüggen Wing went: 67 and 71 in April 1957 and 112 and 130 in May. In June and July 1957 3 and 234 Squadrons in the Geilenkirchen Wing and 98 Squadron of the Jever Wing were disbanded, followed, on 15 September, by 26 Squadron at Oldenburg.

As part of the last rites, 112 Squadron formed 'The 112 Lonely Sharks Club', a reference to the 'sharks-teeth' markings the squadron had made famous in the Desert Air Force in the Second World War and which were applied to their Sabre and Hunter F.4 aircraft. For a few years the 'Lonely Sharks Club' held reunions at the White Hart at Brasted in Kent but ex-Hunter pilots soon became few and far between and the club folded, although 112 Squadron was re-formed as a Bloodhound missile unit on 1 August 1960.

Some of 74 Squadron's Hunter 6s (XE559/D, 'J', 'B', XF502/K, 'E', 'O', XE591/G and XK141/F) lined up at Horsham St Faith, just prior to an AOC's inspection in 1957. Flg Off Ian Cadwallader recalls: 'Believe it or not all the pilots had to turn to and clean them! All the senior pilots on the squadron had their name on an aircraft and this was a great incentive to keep an eye on your a/c and make sure during normal operations that oil and fuel stains etc. were cleaned off. The 6s were brand new when we got them and the paintwork was beautiful. I had my name on 'F-Foxtrot'. Cadwallader's aircraft (XK141/F) had been delivered in August that year, and served later with 229 OCU. In October 1976 it moved to the TWU at Brawdy, transferring to Lossiemouth with 2 TWU in 1979. (*Ian Cadwallader*)

Another view of the line-up. In the background are two Avro Ansons, in which the AOC and his staff arrived, and a Bristol Sycamore HR13 ASR helicopter of D Flight, 275 Squadron. To relieve the overcrowding caused by the influx of the two Javelin squadrons, D Flight had moved to Coltishall on 12 October 1956 but returned to Horsham St Faith the following month when it was felt that the Sycamores were interfering with construction work. In late May and early June 1959 the Javelin Wing returned to Coltishall, where, on 8 June, they were joined by 74 Squadron's Hunter F.6s, the jet noise at Horsham St Faith, close to Norwich, having become a nuisance to city residents. (Horsham, which was then used by the RAF and a Hawker company working party to convert thirty-six Hunter F.6s to Interim FGA.9 standard, later became Norwich Airport!) On the night of 25/6 August 1959 XF502/K (second left) and XF425/H collided shortly after take-off from Coltishall. Flt Lt Peter Rayner ejected safely from XF425, which descended in flames. Despite a search by a SAR Sycamore with a searchlight, the body of Flg Off Peter Budd was not found. He was finally discovered in the wreckage of XF502 the next morning. (*Ian Cadwallader*)

'The squadron was taken over by Sqn Ldr C.J. Homes. Homes, who had come straight from the Air Ministry, gave the pilots a talk on the development of the fighter aircraft after which there was a "deathly silence". The reason for this silence was that current forward thinking concerning the interception of enemy aircraft in the future could only be done by guided missiles and that manned fighters would soon be obsolete. It seemed as though the writing was on the wall. "All sorts of rumours wandering around, engendered by the official political talk of economies in the forces and withdrawing troops from NATO. People say that squadrons will be disbanded, there shortly won't be jobs for anyone . . . one can't help feeling that fighter squadrons as we know them today will soon be a thing of the past . . ." On 1 March 1957 a few telephone calls produced a "Balbo" of sixteen aircraft – eight from 112, five from 67 and three from 3 Squadron at Geilenkirchen – which flew south over the American Zone. Led by A Flight commander, the formation flew at contrail height in order to scramble the F-86 Dogs for a huge aerial combat. In the past this had brought up every kind of jet fighter from the USAF airfields near the Mosel but on this occasion they seemed unwilling to mix it, much to everyone's disappointment. Group was interested to hear how we got on when we returned and the Wg Cdr Flying was happy. Had the Brüggen Wing continued in existence there were plans to repeat the performance.'

Flt Lt Robin A. Brown, Hunter F.4 pilot, Shark Squadron:
The History of 112 Squadron, 1917–1975, Crecy, 1994

Thursday 16 May 1957, the anniversary of 112's re-forming in 1939, was the last day that Shark Squadron was operational and Robin Brown led a farewell flypast. The Hunter formation took a route planned so as to overfly as many of the local airfields as possible, namely Laarbruch, Volkel, Eindhoven, Kleine Broghel, Geilenkirchen, HQ 2nd TAF and finally Brüggen itself.

By the end of 1958 all Hunter squadrons in Fighter Command had completed their re-equipment with Hunter F.6s. In January 1958, 208 Squadron was formed with Hunter F.6s at Tangmere, and on 20 March this squadron departed for Nicosia, Cyprus, to join the Middle East Air Force (MEAF). In November 1958, 263 and 56 re-equipped with the Hunter F.6 at Wattisham. In Germany the five F.4 squadrons that remained in 2nd TAF completed re-equipment with Hunter F.6s by mid-1958.

No. 26 Squadron had re-formed at Gütersloh in June 1958 as part of 121 Wing and its Hunter F.6s operated from Ahlhorn until disbandment in December 1960. That same month 93 Squadron at Jever and 20 Squadron at Oldenburg disbanded also. On 31 August 1962, 118 Squadron disbanded at Jever, while 14 Squadron, the last day fighter unit in 2nd TAF, disbanded on 17 December that year. Altogether some 383 Hunter F.6s were supplied to the RAF.

2nd TAF Battle Flight

'I was posted to 93 Squadron in 1956 as my first operational tour. We were equipped with the Hunter Mk 4 and soon after my arrival with the Mk 6. This latter aircraft was a very lively machine. It had no "saw tooth" leading edge, no pylons for external stores and no blast deflectors on the guns. Apart from being a very clean airframe, the engine max RPM was 8,300. After some failures this was later reduced to 7,950, but at the time this aircraft would climb to 40,000ft in about 6 minutes. As a very young, under-confident and immature pilot officer (my rank ribbon was so thin, people would pretend to brush away this "loose thread") I always assumed that most of my exploits would end either in disaster or on the Boss's mat.

'I was tasked one morning as wing-man on "battle flight" (guns armed on the end of the runway), briefed – "start up on Echo and don't drop back" – nobody ever got scrambled on battle flight. This early morning was different and the tower signalled us to go. In the excitement that followed my gallant leader set off down the runway with the red ladder still attached to his left side. I was on his right and unaware of this error. At about 250 knots the ladder came off and jammed in the engine intake. The engine coughed and my leader turned back to land (the good old RR Avon got him back on the ground).

'I changed channels to the fighter control frequency and was told that this was not a practice but a real intruder scramble. As I nervously removed the sticky tape from the guns' safety catch I pondered upon whether as the most junior pilot in the entire Air Force I was about to initiate the Third World War. I was vectored east and told to make maximum height. As I reached 40,000ft I was told the target was at 12 o'clock and 20,000ft above! As I passed 50,000ft the aircraft really started to feel sloppy and eventually at 55,000ft I was on the edge at a high mach no., but very low indicated airspeed. As the East German border approached I was told to reverse course and staggered round on the stall. I looked up and there still way above me was what looked like a large glider, black and, amazingly, moving slower than me. I passed this information to the controller who suddenly became very terse and told me to return to base without delay.

'On landing the wing commander (flying) asked me what I had seen and then told me I was completely mistaken and to forget the whole thing. It was a little while before Khrushchev banged his shoe on the table at the UN in a temper tantrum over some American chap by the name of Gary Powers. I then realized that maybe I had not dreamed up my trip to the tropopause.'

Plt Off Roger E. Hymans (later a flight lieutenant and a member of the Black Arrows team)

At Hawkers the crisis of confidence caused by Sandys' White Paper was largely overcome with the introduction of the ground-attack Hunter, of which more later, and F.4 production was further increased in the late 1950s and early 1960s to meet the needs of several overseas air forces. In February 1955 a Hunter F.4 was bought by Sweden, which in June 1954 had placed an order for 120 J.34 (Hunter 50s) to be built at Blackpool. Production of the Mk 50 continued until 1958 and the Swedish Flygvapnet operated the type until 1966. Denmark followed with orders for 30 Mk 51s and 2 T.53 trainer aircraft, which were also based on the F.4 airframe. The first Mk 51 was delivered on 30 January 1956, the Kongelige Dansk Flyvevaben operating Hunters until 31 March 1974. Similarly, 16 Hunter 52s were purchased by Peru and delivered in early 1956. A two-seat Hunter was dispatched to Peru in 1959. Hawkers used 32 aircraft from the cancelled RAF order to help meet a 1956 order from India for 160 Hunter 56s (F.6s). Withdrawing F.6s from RAF service for refurbishment produced the next 16 single-seat Hunters for India. By 1960 the entire order (22 Mk 66 two-seat Hunters were also ordered) had been fulfilled. In 1966 India ordered 53 Mk 56A aircraft (and 12 T.66Ds) to make up losses sustained in the war with Pakistan in 1965. An order for 5 T.66Es (conversions of RAF F.6s) followed.

In 1958, meanwhile, Switzerland had ordered 100 Hunter 58s for the Flugwaffe after 2 F.6s had successfully beaten competing designs in trials in 1957. Again, some of the cancelled MoS order was used, and Switzerland had received all the aircraft ordered by April 1960. Switzerland followed this with an order in 1969 for another 30 single-seat Hunters and 8 two-seat T.68s, for delivery during 1971–3. By the mid-1970s Hawkers had reaped a rich dividend from the small but steady sales of refurbished ex-RAF, Dutch and Belgian Hunters for air forces in Africa and the Middle East (Rhodesia, Kuwait, Jordan, Lebanon, Iraq, Abu Dhabi, Qatar, Kenya, Oman and Saudi Arabia). Fokker in Holland and Avions Fairey in Belgium built the Hunter F.4 under licence. All told, 96 Dutch F.4s were built (followed later by 93 F.6s) while Belgium built 111 F.4s (and 144 F.6s). Orders were also received from South America (Chile) and the Far East (Singapore), in addition to the repeat business from India and Switzerland. All this activity helped fund other projects, not least of which was the highly successful P.1127 Kestrel/Harrier series.

Despite the RAF cut-backs, life on the Hunter stations such as Horsham St Faith went on much the same, with exercises being flown frequently. It was not unusual for the weather to cause problems, as Bob Cossey, the noted 74 'Tiger' Squadron historian, recalls:

The weather during March 1958 was particularly severe, a blizzard blowing on the first day of spring, but, in spite of the intense cold, during the rest of the month flying conditions were very good and over 500 hours were clocked up – the best month so far on Hunters. Daily flying included dogfighting – one vs. one and two vs. two – which was legal if briefed (that is not to say that it did not happen otherwise!) and would start at high level and finish at a minimum of 5,000ft. Chris Curtis and later Pete Carr, together with the USAF's Jack Martin (the latest American exchange officer), spent a lot of time working on tactics and impressed the Day Fighter Leader School with some of the results! The 'sliding attack', for example, was evolved for use against the Russian Bears and Bisons with their rearward-facing guns. It was discovered that there was a blind spot which the bombers' guns could not reach without damaging their own tails, so the attacking aircraft would position itself 2,000yds ahead and to one side of the aircraft, flying in the same direction. It would turn in 20 degrees and drift towards it in its blind spot, opening fire at 200–300yds, raking the wing with fire from the Aden gun. The tactic, practised frequently in Hunter vs. Hunter exercises, was considered far preferable to creeping up behind the enemy in the vulnerable position.

Heightened tension in Cyprus, Jordan and the Lebanon in mid-1958 saw 208 Squadron leave Tangmere for Nicosia in March. They were often supported by detachments from other Hunter squadrons in the UK. Terry Kingsley, a Hunter pilot in 66 Squadron, recalls:

When I finally made it to the Akrotiri base, the rest of the squadron were already set up in the dispersal areas, ready for conflict. They needed able bodies, and in my winter flying clothing I was quickly sitting in a Hunter on alert in the hot sun. The aircraft were not equipped with hot-weather cooling units, and the temperate ones soon failed under the strain, leaving us without any cockpit air-conditioning. We had no time to acclimatize, and fatigue rapidly became a factor. Temperatures were so high that the metal of the seat harness blistered one's shoulders. I sweated so much on one sortie that the fluorescein sea marker – the green dye used in life jackets – leaked out and dyed me a brilliant green.

With the build-up of forces, space became a priority. We moved to Nicosia, the civil airfield in the centre of the island. Here living conditions were very cramped for a time, with crews living in the squash court. I was sharing a chalet with a RAF regiment officer, whose work schedule rarely coincided with mine.

The Turkish/Greek troubles were heating up, so much so that we only employed Turkish workers on the base. The Greeks had blown up a fuel truck at Akrotiri, and a Canberra had been damaged. We rarely left the base area, and we were armed or escorted if we did.

The US landed on the beach at Beirut, but all in all operations were conducted with virtually no co-operation. The Israelis demanded, quite rightly, that overflights of their country cease, for all the British force had to overfly Israel, and we did. The US FJ3s landed at Nicosia and displayed their Sidewinder missiles. These were the first that we had seen close up, but there was little or no collaboration.

We were alerted early one morning and called to the squadron area for a briefing. Survival kits were handed out, including gold coins and the venerable 'goolie chits'. These and the silk maps were supposed to give some measure of comfort in some very hostile territory. Whether the natives would actually accept a chit was in doubt, but we did have the Smith & Wesson option. The mission included arming the Hunters with long-range tanks and guns

only, for the target was at extreme range. I later learned that it was a one-way mission with no hope of making the return flight. No doubts were raised, and I have no fear that, had the order been given, all fourteen aircraft would have left without a qualm.

We covered the landings in Amman and were constantly on the lookout for Egyptian aircraft. I was airborne and vectored to a target which proved to be a fleeing Il-28, an outdated Russian bomber. On 22 May 1958 John Davis and I were scrambled after a target coming up from the south. We knew that Egyptian aircraft regularly sneaked in between Cyprus and Israel, bound for Syria. They were obviously more scared of the Israelis than they were of us. Our concern was a sneak attack, thus the rapid response. We climbed as fast as possible to 40,000ft, but could not find the target. In those days height-finding radar was the weak link. Slowly we descended, searching at each level. Finally at 8,000ft we identified an Il-14M, a Russian-made transport. He was flying north heading for Cyprus, or the gap. I sat on his wing to gather some specifics for the now very interested controller at the radar station. It was a shiny new aircraft, with an amazing series of insignia on the tail – big stars, half-moons, obviously a VIP transport. I could see clearly into the cockpit, and there appeared to be nobody on the aircraft. I pushed in closer and both pilot seats were unoccupied. By now, the controller was getting excited. All controllers had a numbered call sign, and we had been controlled by a lowly number like 28. A new controller would come on the air, announce his call sign and request the same data all over again. Slowly the more senior numbers came up, until finally it was 01 himself. This was the sector commander who could smell an international incident brewing.

John D. sat back and finally came in to verify my assessment of the situation. The Il-14 was slowing almost imperceptibly, and it was flying at the stalling speed of the Hunter. We had gear and flaps down and were very vulnerable in that condition. Fuel was becoming a serious concern, but Control would not release us. In a few minutes we would not have enough fuel to be able to return to Nicosia. I looked at the Il-14 and nearly spun in laughing as I made out a pair of very bushy black eyebrows peering over the edge of the cockpit windowsill. The crew must have been lying on the floor, operating the autopilot.

The aircraft closed in to Cypriot airspace and we were unable to get any instructions on dealing with it. I realized that the system was just not able to respond and knew that we needed much clearer rules of engagement, something that the US had enormous trouble with much later in Vietnam. The following day the incident was reported in the world press as piracy in the air, and needless to say all our cine film was removed pronto. The Il-14M was a gift to Nasser from Khruschev.

After taking part in the long-running series of Kingpin air defence exercises, 74 Squadron was placed on short notice alert as a direct result of the increased tension in Lebanon, and on 8 September 1958 the 'Tigers' flew to Cyprus. Twelve-day cycles comprising four days on battle flight, four days on squadron training, three days on stand-down and one day 'at the Squadron Commander's disposal' were carried out. Crews also flew a large number of low-level strike sorties using 2-inch rockets and cannon, as well as Army cooperation work and air-to-air firing on the Larnaca range. In October 74 Squadron provided protection for the daily supply convoy travelling between Famagusta and the GCA station at Cape Greco. This convoy had suffered many ambushes by EOKA terrorists. Arthur Bennett recalls:

> We flew figures of eight at 100ft as slowly as possible just ahead of the convoy, with the aim of spotting anyone who might be setting up an ambush. As it happened, a suspect was caught on the very first morning, having been seen by Chris Curtis. That was the only incident, and the flights were discontinued after two or three days anyway as they were potentially quite hazardous, both from the point of view of presenting an easy target for ground fire as well as the risks of flying low and slow.
>
> [A detachment of five aircraft went to El Adem for four days.] This was also interesting as it provided a useful opportunity to do some low flying over the Libyan Desert. However, the main purpose of the detachment was to deter the Egyptians from sending Il-28 Beagle reconnaissance flights over Libyan territory. In the event we did have one scramble and interception but the target turned out to be a civilian

The 74 Squadron 'Roller' was donated to the 'Tigers' by Nick Tester's father after his son's death on 21 August 1958 in Hunter F.6 XF448/N. Flg Off Ian Cadwallader recalls what happened: 'Nick was flying behind me in a three-aircraft tail chase and for some unexplained reason he dived from quite a high altitude straight into the North Sea just off the coast near Yarmouth.' A full air and sea search was initiated, in what was one of the biggest rescue operations mounted locally for many years. Tester's colleagues themselves flew until dusk, but apart from oil slicks nothing was sighted. Diving operations were subsequently started at the marked position of one of the slicks but, again, nothing was found. (*Ian Cadwallader*)

T.7 XL568/X of 74 Squadron at Horsham St Faith on a cold day in March 1959. This aircraft first flew on 6 March 1958 and was delivered to the 'Tigers' on 20 October 1958. In 1963 it was converted to Hunter T.7A and in 1971 was assigned to 237 OCU. (*Ian Cadwallader*)

aircraft of the Il-14 type. The pilot was most unhappy about the interception and complained bitterly to all and sundry over the distress frequency when our aircraft drew up alongside.

Early in November 1958, 74 Squadron returned home. The year 1959 was notable for yet more exercises and a new CO, Sqn Ldr Peter Carr, took over from Sqn Ldr Chris Curtis in July. Pete Carr recalls:

I was posted from the AFDS at West Raynham where we were lucky enough to evaluate the Mks 4, 5 and 6, the F.6 being in use at 74 Squadron when

I joined them. The only criticism to be levelled against the Hunter in the 1960s was that it hadn't enough outright speed to deal with the likely bomber and fighter threat. Apart from the fundamental advantage that reheat would have given, the addition of Sidewinder missiles would have been a great help in the short term, but no doubt the Air Ministry had decided that such expenditure was unnecessary in view of the impending arrival of the Lightning.

In 1960 all eyes in the RAF were on the new supersonic fighter. The first three pre-production examples had already been built and delivered to the AFDS at Coltishall for initial operational

T.7 XL605/T of 92 Squadron, pictured at dawn during APC in Nicosia in 1959. XL605 flew for the first time on 14 October 1958 and was delivered to 92 Squadron on 1 December that year. Later it joined 66 Squadron and on 6 April 1966 was purchased by Hawker Siddeley Aircraft for conversion to Saudi Arabian Hunter T.70 (70/617), being delivered on 7 June 1966. In July 1974 XL605 returned to the RAF and was issued to 229 OCU as XX467. In 1976 the two-seater joined the TWU and was numbered '92'! (*Brian Allchin*)

Pilots of 92 Squadron in front of F.6 XF520/K at APC in Nicosia in June 1959. Far right is Flg Off Jeremy Seavers, in the centre is the OC Sqn Ldr Dixon and fourth from right is Flt Lt George Aylett. Hawker Siddeley Aircraft purchased XF520 in June 1966 for conversion to Jordanian FGA.73 (814). (*Brian Allchin*)

No. 92 Squadron line-up at Nicosia, Cyprus, in 1959. In the middle are F.6s XG234/E and XG231/A, while a gun-pack is about to be hoisted into XE532/L. This aircraft was returned to Hawker Siddeley Aircraft on 5 November 1964 for conversion to FGA.9 before being delivered to 8 Squadron. It crashed while serving with 2nd TAF on 6 May 1968. The pilot survived. (*Brian Allchin*)

F.6 WW593 of 92 Squadron pictured in 1959. This was the second of the first production batch of seven aircraft built with Pre-Modification 228 Mk 4 wings by Hawkers at Kingston. Frank Bullen flew it for the first time on 19 August 1955 and Hawkers and the A&AEE used it for miscellaneous trial installations. WW593 was returned to HSA in 1960 for conversion to FR.10 and was delivered on 26 April 1961. (*Brian Allchin*)

Flg Off Brian Allchin in the cockpit of Flt Lt A.H. Back AFC's F.6 XG231/A at Nicosia in June 1959. Note the gun blast deflectors. (*Brian Allchin*)

XG186/J, XG234/E and XG232/G of 92 Squadron taking off at Nicosia in 1959. XG186 was purchased by Hawker Siddeley Aircraft on 6 October 1967 and converted to Indian Hunter 56A (A941), being delivered on 22 March 1969. XG234 was purchased by Hawker Siddeley Aircraft on 9 May 1968 and converted to Jordanian Hunter FGA.73A (830), being delivered on 22 July 1969. XG232 was purchased by HSA on 21 June 1966 for conversion to Chilean FGA.71 (J-714), being delivered on 19 June 1958. (*Brian Allchin*)

evaluation and in January 1960 Sqn Ldr Pete Carr was told that 74 Squadron would be the first to equip with the type in June. However, the CO would not see the new aircraft into service, as he recalls:

> I applied for premature retirement and transfer to the Reserve in March 1960 as I had made the decision to join Donald Campbell as reserve driver and project director for his Land Speed Record attempt in Utah. The decision was very difficult and my appetite had already been whetted for the Mach 2 machine, having had a few rides in the P.1B while serving at AFDS. However, the die had been cast as Donald had already written to the Air Council requesting my release from the RAF as he considered the project would create a favourable image of British industry and the UK.

The South African Sqn Ldr (later AVM) John Howe took Pete Carr's place as the 'Tigers'' Boss.

Not all the Hunter squadrons survived. In September 1960, 66 Squadron at Acklington disbanded, to re-form later as a helicopter squadron. At Wattisham, in January and April 1961 respectively, 56 and 111 ('Treble One') Squadrons became the second and third in RAF Fighter Command to exchange Hunter F.6s for the Lightning F.1A. In April 65 Squadron at Duxford disbanded. This left just five Hunter squadrons – nos 1, 19, 43, 54 and 92 – in Fighter Command. In June 1961, 43 Squadron relocated to Cyprus to come under Near East Command, and in December that same year 1 and 54 Squadrons transferred to 38 Group, Transport Command. At Leconfield 19 Squadron operated the Hunter F.6 until February 1963 and 92 Squadron retained its Hunter F.6s until April 1963, both re-equipping with the Lightning F.2. The Hunter F.6's passing left many legacies, not least the two famous Hunter aerobatic display teams, the Black Arrows of 111 Squadron and the Blue Diamonds of 92 Squadron.

CHAPTER 4

THE BLACK ARROWS

O n 23 January 1955, 34-year-old Sqn Ldr (later Air Cdre) Roger L. Topp AFC* took command of 111 Squadron. At this time it was equipped with Meteor F.8s, but in June it re-equipped with Hunter F.4s. Topp had joined the RAF in 1939 and learned to fly in Canada in 1943 before returning to England in 1944; a surplus of powered aircraft pilots saw him transferred to the Glider Pilot Regiment. On 24 March 1945 he flew a Horsa in the airborne crossing of the Rhine. In 1947 Topp joined 98 Squadron, flying Mosquitos in Germany for three years and becoming a flight commander. In 1950 he attended the ETPS at Farnborough and then spent three years on test-pilot duty, including flight testing the Comet I airliner following its series of accidents. On 8 August 1956 he established a new Edinburgh–London speed record, flying the 331.6 miles from RAF Turnhouse to RAF Northolt in 27 minutes 52.8 seconds at an average speed of 717.504mph in Hunter F.4 WT739/R. (This record stood until July 1987 when two F.4J Phantoms of 74 Squadron, making a rolling start over the North Sea, shattered the record.) In November 1956 'Treble One' received new F.6s with the 'saw tooth' wing and a more powerful engine which enhanced the Hunter's already excellent handling and performance characteristics.

'Treble One' had re-formed on Meteor F.8 jets at North Weald in 1953 and the squadron's interest in formation aerobatics began in 1955. Following re-equipment on Hunters it progressed through a competition in 1956 open to all Fighter Command squadrons flying four-man teams. The two best teams were invited to work up a team to fly at air displays at home and abroad. 'Treble One' provided RAF Fighter Command's reserve team. Flg Off George P. Aird recalls:

The Aerobatic Team began with the Meteor F.8 and continued during the conversion on to the Hunter. The first four members were Sqn Ldr Roger Topp (leader), Flg Off Dave Goodwin (No. 2), myself (No. 3 and deputy leader) and Flt Sgt Bill Beck (No. 4). Later two spares, Flg Off Dave Garratt and Sgt Roy Tappenden, were added. The team continued to grow, with five in 1956 and nine aircraft at the 1957 SBAC show.

For the first time since the war a RAF aerobatic team was permitted to paint its aircraft in a special display finish. After several schemes had been tried, black was chosen, not just because it was part of 111 Squadron's traditional markings, first adopted in 1925, but also because, as Roger Topp explains:

I'd remembered that during the war matt-black instead of camouflage had changed the whole appearance of the night-fighter and made it look a meaner and more impressive aircraft. I had a good personal relationship with ACM Sir Thomas Pike, AOC RAF Fighter Command, and he agreed that

The Black Arrows practising a twenty-one Hunter formation at RAF Wattisham in the summer of 1958. At SBAC Farnborough in September the team, led by Sqn Ldr Roger Topp, performed the famous twenty-two loop in public for the first time. (*Tony Aldridge*)

I could try out one of the Hunters in black. Cellon Paints didn't do matt black but they painted one gloss black especially for us. Sir Tom then gave us the OK for five to be painted black. He demurred when I asked to let us paint four more, but with Farnborough coming up, we just quietly did it!

A leading French commentator, describing their display at Bordeaux on 12 May 1956, had referred to the team as 'les Flèches Volantes' ('the Flying Arrows'). Now, a year later, they had become accepted universally, courtesy of remarks in a French newspaper following the 22nd Paris Aeronautical Salon display of 1 June 1957, as 'les Flèches Noir' – the 'Black Arrows'. As Roger Topp says, 'That was good enough for us!'

The 1957 Paris Aeronautical Salon display at Le Bourget saw the keenest rivalry between the four national teams on the programme. (The Black Arrows were the only team in Europe regularly flying five swept-wing aircraft.) After one team had earned special applause for its formation landing with four aircraft, Roger Topp quickly modified his team's normal landing procedure and led a formation of five in to land together instead

'From early in 1956 to 1960 I was part of a team of four in a Contractors Working Party (CWP) at North Weald, and at times, 30 to 40 Hunters were parked on the airfield awaiting their turn to be modified. In addition there were the Hunters belonging to 111 Squadron – the famous Black Arrows. They flew all day and every day whenever weather was good. The sky always seemed to have at least one Hunter in it. Black Hunters with white smoke trails against a pure blue sky was very dramatic, incredible sight.

'Unfortunately there were two crashes while I was there. On 30 April 1957 ACM Sir Harry Broadhurst, then C-in-C Bomber Command, presented the colours to 111 Squadron. After the ceremony, a flying display was given by five 111 Squadron black Hunters, following which they did a stream landing. North Weald runway has an awkward bump in it and if you catch it just slightly wrongly it makes you bounce. The last Hunter of the five [XG203/H, flown by Flg Off Michael Thurley] caught the bump and started a kangaroo-type bounce which got higher and slower every time, ending with an enormous crash and explosion at the far end of the runway. It was the sort of crash no one can survive, we thought. However, when the dust and smoke cleared, there was the pilot picking himself up in the overshoot area. I was probably second to the pilot in breathing a massive sigh of relief. The final plunge to earth was sufficiently bad to break the front from the centre fuselage and that same impact drove the ejection seat up the rail and fired it. The seat, complete with pilot, landed in the ploughed overshoot area, separating as it hit the ground. XG203 was a write-off and completely burnt out. Fortunately, the pilot was able to walk away; he escaped with some minor back injuries but was fit to fly another day. [Thurley was taken to St Margaret's Hospital, Epping, and was back with the team just three weeks later.]

'We lost another 111 Squadron aircraft on 8 June 1957, when the squadron carried out extensive aerobatic practice with a formation of five aircraft. Flg Off Dave Garrett, piloting XF525, and Flt Lt 'Straw' Hall, flying XE621, collided and Garrett crashed on the airfield adjacent to ASF Hangar and he was killed. XE621, with a 5ft section of its port wing bent up, managed to stagger to Stansted Airport, and made a high-speed landing. It was declared Cat 4 and returned to Hawkers, Blackpool, for repair, before re-entering RAF service in February 1959.'

Eric Hayward, Hawker CWP, North Weald, 1957

The cartridge had fired the seat out of the aircraft and a combination of the correct angle of ejection and the fact that the seat caught the side of the cockpit (which reduced the acceleration) allowed the pilot to land softly. The fuselage was rolling over at the time and a fraction of a second earlier or later would have caused Thurley to either go straight up into the air or peg straight into the ground.

The Black Arrows of 111 Squadron at Wattisham in 1958. (*Tony Aldridge*)

The Black Arrows practising twenty-two-formation aerobatics, 1958. (via *Tony Aldridge*)

Signing autographs at the May 1958 Earls Court exhibition. Sqn Ldr Roger Topp AFC** is in the centre of the photograph with fellow Black Arrows pilots, from left (standing), Mike Thurley, Les Swart, Paddy Hine and (seated) Bob Barcillon.

of heading the normal stream landing. The result was that, once again, they stole the show and were accorded even greater applause.

One of the team's many performances was from Odiham before live television cameras. It was a brief appearance and the timing had to be, if possible, slicker than ever. Everything seemed set fair on the run in for the show. Then, as they appeared within range of the cameras, Topp discovered that his radio had failed. He could neither send nor receive. Topp decided he would fly the rehearsed pattern, leaving the aircraft in box formation without any changes. Aird, his deputy, immediately sensed what had gone wrong. He knew the planned sequence of the manoeuvres and so proceeded to 'call the changes'. The show went off without a hitch and was as neat as ever. (In January 1958 Aird was posted to 229 OCU at RAF Chivenor as an instructor, having been on 111 Squadron for four years – the normal tour was 2½ years. He left the RAF in March 1959 to become a test pilot for de Havilland's at Hatfield, where, on 13 September 1962, he ejected from Lightning XG332.)

Aerobatic techniques were improved and the year 1958 brought fresh triumphs. Also in that year 'Treble One' moved, first to North Luffenham as a detachment on 19 February, then to Wattisham in Suffolk on 16 June. Jet-pipe smoke generators were fitted to the aircraft, and thus the team was able to produce bold smoke trails to trace the pattern of its manoeuvres. Roger Topp, who in January was awarded a second bar to his AFC, recalls:

We went through the same motions as in 1957 – what are we going to do this year? We heard rumours of the large number being flown by other air forces but that's all they were, rumours. We thought of a sixteen formation – our squadron's full complement of aircraft – but then felt that we could make a really big impact at Farnborough in September with something even larger. In fact, without Sir Tom's personal backing, we could never have built up the team to the twenty-two loop . . . Lots of weird and

wonderful shapes were considered, and tried. I would think of a shape and then fly some kind of envelope; perhaps half of it, on one side, putting in five and then two more behind, to prove the theory. You can do this many times, over many shapes. We played around and eventually came up with twenty-one (seven echelons of three). This was fine but there was something missing. I decided that the centre 'stem' should be a little longer, so we added one.

It all took enormous organization and planning and the ground staff had to get twenty-six Hunters serviceable as required. Sqn Ldr Mike Hobson recalls:

I was commanding 92 Squadron at RAF Middleton St George when Roger put forward his somewhat staggering proposal to loop twenty-two Hunters over Farnborough. Since this number of aircraft was obviously way beyond 111's resources, the Powers-That-Be proposed, quite rightly, that other squadrons in Fighter Command should contribute sufficient aircraft. [Topp requested and obtained, eight Hunters and pilots from other squadrons, CFE and 229 OCU for the event to make up the number, plus adequate spares.] No. 92 Squadron's contribution was two aircraft which were eventually prised out of me despite much mumbling in my beard about my squadron's operational training being sacrificed for the sake of somebody else's publicity gimmick – the aircraft were required for quite a long period for preparation and practice beforehand. This, of course, was really nothing but a case of sour grapes, for we all realised that the 'publicity gimmick' could do nothing but good for the name of the Service!

Roger Topp takes up the story:

'"TREBLE ONE" Squadron have what is surely the finest aerobatic team the Royal Air Force or any other Air Force has ever known. Their show delights the layman and exhilarates the connoisseur . . . As well as the team's practical value in terms of prestige, showing the flag, recruitment, squadron spirit and so on, it is immensely satisfying for all of us to watch these sparkling demonstrations of men and machinery combining for our great delight.'
Wren, 'Topp Team', The Aeroplane, 11 July 1958

Not every squadron wanted to give us their 'aces', or their best Hunters, and I could receive pilots who were regarded as 'Black sheep' on their squadrons and some of the aircraft which might be 'rogues'. We let them come with their aeroplanes and without protest and I think that once they settled down they were very happy. Most pilots in a squadron can fly formation aerobatics, but not all have the personality for exhibition flying. It takes a man with a very stable personality to go to a big air show, engage in competition with other teams and stand up under the stress and strain. You might call it the 'big match temperament'.

The 22-loop was purely a build-up from doing something more than the sixteen. It more or less evolved as we tried to get something that made sense to look at, had impact and was feasible to fly. Twenty-two aircraft provided a spare aircraft within the formation. If it was used it meant I wouldn't have to call in a spare from elsewhere. (Although I would have two airborne spares, one over Aldershot and one over Camberley, once you were committed to the run-in there was no way you could use them). If we got a failure then the drill was for everyone to just move up their own line, and the 22nd aircraft could fill in the gap.

Flg Off Tony M. Aldridge, born in Edinburgh, had been a pilot in the Southern Rhodesian Air Force for over two years before coming to England. He joined 'Treble One' in October 1957, straight from his Hunter conversion course at Chivenor. He recalls the intensive training for the 22-formation display at Farnborough 1958:

At Wattisham on 12 August we did a 21-loop, and on 14 August we did the 22-loop for the first time. We joined up numbered in strings 1-2-3-4, then 2-1, 2-2, 2-3, 3-1, 3-2, 3-3, etc., (I was 7-2) so that there were three in each column except the centre one, which was four. The formation was so long from front to back that when the boss was going down and his aircraft was accelerating, we at the back, who were still climbing, had difficulty keeping up. This was a perpetual problem. When Mick Chase, a superb Air Ministry photographer, took a photo which proved this, we realized corrective action was needed, so at the top of the loop the boss relaxed the back pressure on the stick to allow us to keep position. We practised the 22-loop twice a day for four days, 26–9 August, at Odiham, where we were based for Farnborough week.

The Black Arrows on the pan at Wattisham in 1958 with Javelins of 41 Squadron. (*Tony Aldridge*)

Five Black Arrows in line abreast formation in 1958. (*Air Ministry*)

On Monday 1 September the team practised in the morning and gave their first display that afternoon in front of 7,300 VIPs and guests in the trade stands. An ominous pall of black smoke in the distance towered skywards from the direction of Farnborough as the team taxied out. Palls of black smoke usually meant someone had crashed. Flg Off Tony Aldridge again: 'It was a fairly tense occasion. Everyone 'gulped!' It turned out that a Sea Hawk FGA.6 from the RN 'Hawks' display team had a fire in the cockpit. The pilot, Lt Dimmock, ejected and suffered a broken ankle.

Flight waxed lyrical:

Fast closing from the North [sic] comes a field of Hunters reined as one – Treble One's Twenty-two . . . Rearing up they disclose themselves in three impeccable chevrons of seven, and continue up and over to complete the most wonderful mass aerobatic manoeuvre ever witnessed at Farnborough (or, we

are moved to declare, elsewhere). And this is no mere one-off, call-it-a-day flash-in-the-pan; simply the first half of a double loop – and the first glimpse of a Treble One performance transcending all others . . .

On Tuesday, 'the sight of 22 Hunters, all in a broad vic and all in a loop, could not fail to impress', reported *Flight*, adding, 'and the RAF were, if anything, in better form than on Monday'. On 'wet Wednesday' the cloud base at Odiham was only 300ft, in spite of which five Hunters came over to make the most of patchy weather. The formation's initial loop was completed in cloud and the remainder of the display comprised banked flypasts in changing formations during a series of wide circuits. Back to full strength again, the formation gave another splendid display on Thursday, 'the Hunters cutting across the sun's rays edging over a cloud to give a

Opposite: The Black Arrows practising an experimental 'threading the needle/bomb burst' at Wattisham in 1958. This experiment was not carried forward to the display routine. (*Tony Aldridge*)

The Black Arrows waiting to roll at Farnborough in September 1959. Note the two 'borrowed' and camouflaged Hunters in the line-up, the one far right probably being flown by Flg Off William R. 'Dick' Clayton-Jones ('T' behind). These two were used as the airborne spares. (via *Adrian Balch*)

The Black Arrows, F.6 XE653/F nearest, taxi out in pairs at Farnborough on 13 September 1959. XE653 first flew on 6 July 1956 in the hands of David Lockspeiser, and it was delivered on 24 August to 5 MU before service with 43 and 111 Squadrons. It transferred to 229 OCU in June 1964 and from 1977 served with the Tactical Weapons Unit. (via *Adrian Balch*)

subtle, flickering shadow pattern. The finale, on Sunday, was in front of 110,000 people.'

Some 5 miles out from Farnborough the two spares returned to Odiham as planned and as Topp says:

We ran in at 150ft, right to the end of the runway, where I initiated pull-up for the straight loop. When entering a formation loop from level flight it is not always easy for the pilots to keep station because of summer turbulence, but once we got 'G' on, the formation settled down. At the top of the loop I relaxed the back pressure on the stick, flew almost inverted at around 120 knots, and paused until in my mirror I saw the wings of the fourth aircraft in the stem. When those behind topped the rise I started easing down. Descending with 'G' lessened the effect of the 'bumps', and at the bottom we flew a second, tighter and neater, loop. I then shed six aircraft [5-3, 7-2 and 7-3 (port) and 4-3, 6-2 and 6-3 (starboard)] and barrel-rolled to port the remaining diamond sixteen in formation before shedding a further seven. The diamond nine then looped before four bomb-burst away, leaving a standard box five, which I could fly like one aeroplane. We performed a variety of formation patterns as tight and with as much 'G' as I liked, with the spectacular Prince of Wales feathers finale to finish.

Mike Hobson concludes:

As we all now know, Roger and his team did a superb job, and the feat has gone down in history. When all the shouting was over, and the surplus aircraft were returned to their rightful owners, I received my two 92 Squadron aircraft back resplendent in Treble One's colours! All good inter-squadron rivalry, I suppose. I had not met Roger at the time, but we became good friends, and some eight years later I was lucky enough to take over from him the finest Station [Coltishall] in the UK.

Most of the season's twenty-four major displays in seven countries, in front of about 2 million spectators, were given with five Hunters.

In October 1958 Roger Topp, who had formed and developed the team, which had gained a worldwide reputation for the skill and precision of its formation aerobatics over three years, was posted and 33-year-old Sqn Ldr (later AVM) Peter A. Latham AFC took command of the squadron at Wattisham. Fourteen of the pilots from whom the 1958 Hunter display team was selected now remained. Latham had the responsibility for building, from these 'veterans', a team capable of maintaining the squadron's high reputation in international formation aerobatics. He introduced coordinated displays with two teams, one of nine and the other of five or seven, the smaller team being led by Flt Lt (later Sqn Ldr) Brian Mercer, the deputy leader. It was thus possible to get in more manoeuvres in less time, and on one occasion the Black Arrows gave no fewer than seven shows at different places in one day.

The Black Arrows gave fifty-five displays in 1959, thrilling crowds as far afield as Goodwood,

'The job offers a challenge to be the complete master of the machine. In the same way you find that the squadron pilots are good car drivers and keen on maintaining their cars in good condition. Aerobatic work is applied flying. It is like learning Latin at school. It may not have any direct relationship with what you do later. But it is part of your general education. Give a pilot an air-firing problem and his skill acquired in aerobatic training may come in very useful. . . . We must kick up a terrific din and one would think the local people might feel annoyed about it. But instead of complaints we receive compliments and gentle criticism of our manoeuvres. The villagers of Bildeston in particular are in the line of fire, but from the grocer and the garage man, from everyone we meet, we receive the friendliest of greetings.'

Sqn Ldr (later AVM) Peter Latham AFC

Latham started his flying career with Cambridge University Air Squadron but late in the war there were too many pilots and the RAF put him to work as a lorry driver! He did not finish his flying training until 1946.

Coventry (in conjunction with the national Air
Races), Spangdahlem, Orleans, Cardiff and Lille.
For the Paris and Farnborough displays the
squadron advanced to coordinated aerobatics
with two teams, of nine and five at Paris, and
nine and seven at Farnborough, one led by the
CO and the other by Brian Mercer. This cut
down the length of the display, but doubled the
number of aerobatics. On some occasions the

squadron was divided into two teams of nine and
five to give shows at widely separated places. On
Battle of Britain Day, 19 September, 'Treble One'
gave three full shows with nine aircraft; three full
shows with five, and one with nine and five
coordinated, making seven for the day. 'That',
said Pete Latham, 'was a record for us.'

On 9 October 1959 the Black Arrows took
part in the FAI Congress at Barcelona. It was a

Here Come the Black Arrows

'What is it like to fly with the Black Arrows? The team all follow their leader, who is the squadron commander, 33-year-old Sqn Ldr Peter Latham. He announces each move over the radio and the word "GO" tells the pilots when to move. "Diamond nine loop first" announces Latham. The Hunters form into a diamond pattern. They are going to perform a mass loop on this formation. Down go their noses to pick up speed. The crowd rushes toward them. Then Latham orders: "Looping Now."

'"Going down for wineglass loop" announces Latham. "Looping now. Wineglass GO."

'A moment later he calls: "Smoke On. GO." And smoke streams from the Hunters to trail their flight.

'"Diamond 9 – GO" orders Latham. The Hunters re-form Diamond 9. Another manoeuvre, worked out originally on the blackboard, practised in the air until perfect, is under way.

'Shortest distance between the Hunters in a manoeuvre is only 5ft. And their maximum speed in a manoeuvre is 450mph! Loops are carried out at 400mph with their speed dropping to 180mph at the top of the loop. And the Black Arrows are proud of the fact that many times they have performed when the aerobats of other nations have abandoned their performances due to weather conditions . . . A number of Latham's team are only 23 and 24. One, Flg Off Roger Hymans, is only 22. If you've never seen the Black Arrows – watch out for them. It's a real thrill!'

Express Window, *26 September 1959*

T.7 XL610/Z of the Black Arrows taxiing out at RAF Brüggen, Germany, on 3 October 1960. Normally Sqn Ldr Pete Latham AFC flew the two-seater, which gave the squadron a spare aircraft by freeing up a F.6. XL610 was only flown in the lead because this T.7 had a 100 Series Avon while the F.6 had a 200 Series engine, and there was a difference of 2,500lb of thrust. As the lead aircraft this was not a problem, but pilots at the back of the formation needed all the power they could get – sometimes more! XL610 was lost on 7 June 1962 with the Wattisham Station Flight. Both pilots were killed in the crash. (via *Adrian Balch*)

F.6 XF506/X of the Black Arrows of 'Treble One' Squadron with the pennant of Sqn Ldr Pete Latham, the OC, taxiing out at RAF Brüggen, Germany, on 3 October 1960. XF506 was converted to Rhodesian FGA.9 (119) and delivered in 1963. (via *Adrian Balch*)

memorable occasion for almost all the wrong reasons, as Flg Off Tony Aldridge remembers:

We were waiting to run in for the display and in our holding pattern when the Spanish controller told us to continue holding as they had a problem. This situation lasted quite a while and eventually, just after someone called 'Bingo One', we were cleared to commence the display. 'Bingo' calls were used to advise the formation leader of the fuel state of the pilot with the least fuel. They varied according to circumstances: i.e., on a return to base a long distance away, the figures were set higher – vice versa if you were over your landing field. Normally during aerobatic shows we used 'Bingo 1' as 800lb per side, 'Bingo 2' was when the 'Bingo' lights came on at 650lb per side and 'Joker' was at 400lb per side. Roughly speaking, at 'Bingo 1' you should be heading home, at 'Bingo 2' planning your landings, and at 'Joker' in the circuit . . .

We did the show and landed after the normal bomb burst followed by a looping break. A Spanish

paratroop stick drop had caused the delay. One of the paratroops had snagged his static line on the tailplane of the dropping aircraft and was trailing behind it until he could be untangled, reeled in and flown over the airfield to be dropped out again. The crowd loved it!

In recognition of the quality of its flying, the squadron was proud to receive, on 29 March 1960, the Britannia Challenge Trophy for 1959. Since 1913 this has been awarded by the Royal Aero Club for 'the most meritorious performance in the air during the year'. In 1960, 111 Squadron was selected for the fourth successive year to provide the leading aerobatic team of Fighter Command. By now only seven of the Hunter display team of 1958 remained. In 1961 and 1962, 92 Squadron's Blue Diamonds carried on the proud Hunter tradition.

CHAPTER 5

THE BLUE DIAMONDS

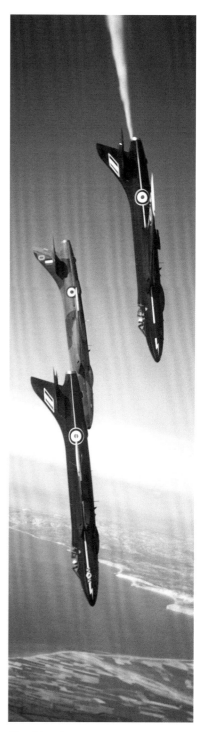

The he Blue Diamonds aerobatic team was provided by 92 Squadron of RAF Fighter Command, a famous unit, which flew Spitfires in the Battle of Britain. By April 1956 it was equipped with the Hawker Hunter F.4, and in 1957 the squadron re-equipped with the F.6, the last of the Hunters used for Day Fighter Ground Attack (DFGA). On 3 October 1960, 32-year-old Sqn Ldr Brian Mercer AFC took command of the squadron at RAF Middleton St George, near Darlington in County Durham, and in 1961 92 Squadron, which on 25 May that year moved to RAF Leconfield, near Beverley in Yorkshire, assumed the main aerobatic commitment of the RAF. 92 Squadron had provided the reserve team to 'Treble One' during the 1960 season and therefore had some experience of aerobatics. To succeed the Black Arrows, one of the world's premier aerobatic teams, and be as good as and preferably better than them was not going to be easy and it required careful planning and excellent leadership. Brian Mercer, who had led the Far East aerobatic team of four Venoms, giving displays at Bangkok and Saigon in 1956, had been the leader of Blue Section of the Black Arrows. Also from the Arrows were Flt Lts Chan Biss, Frank Grimshaw, Tony Aldridge and Chris Strong, most of whom had at least two seasons with 111 Squadron and had taken part in the twenty-two-Hunter loop at Farnborough in 1958.

These five pilots, led by Mercer, formed the core of the Blue Diamonds team, which also included Flt Lts Brian E. St Clair, Ray 'Chips' Carpenter, George Aylett, Derek G. Gill and Flg Off Brian C. Allchin, who had all flown in 92's aerobatic team in 1960. No. 92's other pilots had a mix of experience while one or two were new to the squadron. Flt Lt Pete Taylor was ex 19 Squadron and Flt Lt Don Oakden was formerly on 65 Squadron. Flt Lt Taff Freeman was on his third tour on 92 Squadron. Flt Lt Robbie Roberts was an instructor at RAF Valley. Flt Lt Hamid Anwar, an exchange pilot on No. 92 since July 1960, had participated in the Pakistan Air Force's aerobatic team in 1958. Flt Lt Bill Stoker had joined No. 92 in December 1960 from 26 Squadron and Flg Off Crawford Cameron joined in March 1961. (Cameron was killed in 1962 while practising solo aerobatics at Leconfield.) All were volunteers and experienced pilots.

Flt Lt Tony Aldridge recalls, 'The team had now to get in some serious practice and to this end we were posted to Cyprus in January 1961. After getting back into top form in air-to-ground firing the squadron was posted to RAF Akrotiri for four weeks to train for the aerobatics. During these four weeks the pilots were doing three trips a day – all aerobatics.' At this time, the aircraft acquired their display colours. Tony Aldridge again: 'After a lot of painting models and looking at pictures of aircraft, and checking it did not clash with other

The Blue Diamonds, 'O' still in camouflage, diving out of a loop during formation practice over Cyprus in 1961. (via *Brian Allchin*)

End Plan

'The Black Arrows were a hard act to follow but Brian Mercer had an "end plan", which was to fly a sixteen-ship formation as a normal display. Until Roger Topp arrived on the scene the basic formation team was four. This he increased to five initially, then nine. The 22-loop and 16-roll were a one-off and not something that could be sustained as an aerobatic team. The basic formation was still nine. When Pete Latham took over the Black Arrows he went a bit further, making the full show out of two formations – a nine-ship and a five-ship, i.e. fourteen, with each group performing alternately and joining up at the end with the two spares to carry out a sixteen-aircraft looping break. Brian Mercer's great advance with the Blue Diamonds was to make the basic formation a diamond-sixteen, which was flown in as tight a pattern as a nine-ship. The sixteen-ship performed all the formation manoeuvres that the nine did. This really was the ultimate and no other aero team in the world has ever come close. To make a change from the normal sixteen pattern especially for the SBAC display, after the sixteen-ship part of the show the team split into four by four aircraft formations and performed two manoeuvres, i.e. rolling from each end of the runway and crossing in the middle and then doing four by four bomb bursts in opposing directions. They then rejoined in sixteen echelon for a looping break in four lots of four. They also began the first manoeuvre as four by four ship and then rejoined during the first loop. In the international world of formation aeros none of this had ever been done before and never will be.'

Flt Lt Tony Alldridge

Flying as a Team: Commonwealth Pilots in Senior Aerobatics Squadron

'Three pilots from the Commonwealth overseas are among the handpicked team of experienced RAF aerobatic flyers whose displays are thrilling thousands of people in Britain and Europe. They are Flt Lt Hamid Anwar, from Lyallpur, Pakistan; Flt Lt Tony Aldridge, from Kalomo, Northern Rhodesia; and Hong Kong-born Bill Stoker. All three are twenty-five years of age. They are serving with 92 (East India) Squadron, the Blue Diamonds, in Leconfield, Yorkshire, England.

"When I was posted to 92 Squadron in July 1960", said Flt Lt Anwar, "the squadron was flying as a reserve team to the well-known Black Arrows, which I saw in action at last year's Farnborough show. They were extremely good. But I should say that if we do not keep up the same standard we will go on to do better."

'That is a confident statement to make, but this Pakistani pilot is well able to judge a good squadron when he sees one. Flt Lt Anwar first learnt to fly with No. 2 Punjab University Air Squadron in Lahore. "I have flown aerobatics in Pakistan," he said, "but the training there is not as intensive as it is at this base. I am very happy to be here. My stay with the RAF in Britain for the next year or so will benefit me enormously, and I am sure that the British airmen who are now with the Pakistan Air Force will find their tour of duty just as advantageous."

'One of the "old hands" from the Black Arrow Squadron is Flt Lt Tony Aldridge, who first took to the air in 1953 when he joined the Southern Rhodesia Air Force. After completing his two-year contract, he came to Britain and joined the RAF. "It's a great life," he commented. "Doing aerobatics is completely different from any other sort of flying. It teaches a pilot to handle a plane to its limits."

'Flt Lt Bill Stoker, son of Mr William Stoker, General Manager of the Hong Kong Electric Company, Hong Kong, became keen on flying when he was at school in Scotland. After becoming a private pilot he joined the RAF and was awarded the Flying Prize, the top award of his entry into the training centre at Cranwell.'

magazine article, 1961

An F.6 of 92 Squadron firing its Adens during APC in Cyprus in 1959. (*Brian Allchin*)

Checking the air-to-air target flag for hits! Ducking his head is Flt Lt Chris Strong. To his left is Sqn Ldr Brian Mercer (OC, 92 Squadron). To his right is Flt Lt Derek Gill with his back to the camera, while Flg Off Pete Taylor is stooped, with his hand pointing down. Flt Lt Robbie Roberts is opposite him. John Griffiths, Engineering Officer, is second from right. On the far right is Jeremy Seavers. In Cyprus air-to-air firing was always carried out using coloured tips on the 30-mm cannon shells. Blue, green, red and yellow were normally the colours used. This allowed a section of four to go firing and when the flag came back each score could be checked easily. (*Brian Allchin*)

Armourers loading 4-inch rockets fitted with concrete heads under the starboard wing of F.6 XG137/E of 92 Squadron during the APC in Cyprus, 1959. These rockets were very inaccurate. This aircraft was flown for the first time on 27 August 1956 by David Lockspeiser and was delivered to 19 MU on 18 September that year before being issued to DFLS. Later, it served with 229 OCU and in February 1968 became Jordanian FGA.73 (813). (*Brian Allchin*)

air-force teams in the world, the colour chosen was Royal Blue with white wing tips and a white flash down each side with the squadron checker board on each side of the nose with the cobra rampant in the centre.

In the 1950s and early 1960s the team selected to give aerobatic displays did so while retaining a first-line operational capability. No. 92 Squadron's main role was that of air-defence interception. Its Hunters could also operate in the ground-attack role, and during an operational detachment to Cyprus at the beginning of 1961, when the fine weather was accepted as an opportunity to build up its aerobatic team, it concentrated for four weeks on tactical flying and weapons training. Two weeks were spent solely on air-to-ground firing with 30mm cannon with 60lb rockets carried on rails under the wings.

When a new formation pilot joined the squadron he began by flying in a pair with an experienced man leading him. He learned to fly the three basic positions – echelon, line astern and line abreast. He had to get used to tight turns, wingovers, loops and rolls in those positions. All the time he watched his leader. If flying in No. 2 or No. 3 position immediately adjacent to the leader he lined up his aircraft, by careful use of the throttle and precise manipulation of rudder and ailerons, so that his eyes ran directly along the aileron hinge-line of the leader's Hunter. In line astern the distance can be judged by the pilot's view of the aircraft ahead and experience is a factor. The pilots had to contend with a normal force of 3½ G, with a maximum of 4–5 G. Negative G force was avoided in formation aerobatics though not in individual aerobatics.

The Blue Diamonds looping over Cyprus in 1961. (*Brian Allchin*)

The Blue Diamonds photographed over Cyprus in early 1961 by Flg Off Brian Allchin from the right-hand seat of T.7 XL605/T, piloted by the OC, Sqn Ldr Brian Mercer. The two-seater and XF451 (borrowed from 229 OCU) have yet to be painted in the distinctive blue colour scheme. XF451 was struck off charge after a landing accident on 20 July 1962. (via *Brian Allchin*)

The Blue Diamonds climbing in tight formation over Cyprus in 1961. (via *Brian Allchin*)

As the new man gained more experience he flew in larger formations – of three, then four, then five aircraft – and if the leader was satisfied with his formation-keeping in all attitudes, he would go on to flying in a still larger formation. With the increase in the size of the formation the task is not necessarily a great deal more difficult. The manoeuvres are not quite so tight, the flying is a little more 'gentle', and the main thing is for the pilot to maintain his precise position under all conditions and to get used to the psychological aspect of being surrounded by other aircraft. In a larger formation a pilot must not think solely of his leader – he has to consider also the man flying behind or outside him. Then, as now, it is teamwork that counts.

During a show the Blue Diamonds flew at about 65 per cent of the available power, with 80 per cent for take-off. This power setting was regulated so that the rear men had enough scope to maintain accurate placing: on occasion they may need to have their throttles wide open or right off to stay in position. And the leader had to decide how much power he must put on at any given time so that the rear men have enough margin of power to keep up with him. In a line-abreast formation the further away the aircraft are the more difficult it is to judge distance, and pilots must avoid closing in or opening out ('concertina-ing'). Each lined up his eyes on the leader's cockpit, and with experience could decide if he was the correct distance away.

The speed maintained during a show varied from 150mph to about 460mph. The pilots used 10 degrees of flap all the time to increase the drag and prevent the speed from building up. This helped to tighten the pattern and also to keep the formation within a smaller area, so allowing more manoeuvres to be flown within the specified time. Spectators do not like to keep turning their heads to look all over the sky: a good aerobatic team leader always ensures that his formation is in a position where it can be seen with the minimum effort. Normally a nine-aircraft formation will keep within a radius of 2 miles; with only five aircraft the radius is reduced to 1½ miles, provided that conditions are ideal – that is, with no cloud and no 'bumps'. With a five-aircraft formation the height of the display varied between 500ft and 4,500ft; nine aircraft would go up to 5,000ft. If the wind was strong it was much more difficult to maintain correct positioning in relation to the crowd. When flying down-wind the display pattern had to be tightened; if into wind it was slackened off a little and extended.

The smoke emitted by the Hunters during a show undoubtedly enhanced the effect of a performance. In the Hunter the smoke device, which injected diesel oil into the jet efflux, was carried in the ammunition bay and was so simple a fitting that it could be replaced by a fully armed gun-pack in five minutes. The tank carried 40 gallons of diesel fuel, enough for three minutes' smoking. The release was linked up with the gun-firing circuit so that to turn on the smoke the pilot merely had to press the gun trigger, a system invented by 111 Squadron.

'It was a good time on an aerobatics squadron, but damned hard work. For example, the diesel bowser took the best part of two days to get to Farnborough from Leconfield. The diesel oil was needed on the Hunters to make smoke during displays. Ejecting oil into the jet efflux where it burned created this. The oil was contained in the gun-pack and was operated by the gun trigger on the joystick.'

David Grimer, 92 Squadron

The Blue Diamonds flew a wide variety of formations, with intriguing names such as Diamond Nine, Wine-glass, Delta (sometimes known as the 'Draken', because it resembled the

The Blue Diamonds diving down for a bomb burst over Cyprus in 1961. 'G' is XG232. (via *Brian Allchin*)

Sqn Ldr Brian Mercer AFC* in his vintage Alfa Romeo in front of his Hunter, F.6 XG225/M, at Middleton St George in 1961. XG225 first flew on 20 October 1956, joining 229 OCU in September 1964 and moving to Brawdy in October 1976. (*Brian Allchin*)

Two Blue Diamonds F.6s en route to Tehran, Iran, led by Canberra WJ626 (a Handley Page-built B.2), which was used to provide navigation for the team. (*Brian Allchin*)

plan view of the Swedish fighter of that name), the Half-Swan, Full Swan, Seven Arrow, Box, Line Abreast, Fork and Card Five. Other patterns were possible but, as Mercer said: 'One must beware of changing the form of a display just for the sake of doing something different. Hunter displays have become well established and experience has pointed the way towards what the spectators want to see. A new pattern may not necessarily be better than an existing one, and all the time you have to resist the temptation to make a change.'

It was not unusual for the Blue Diamonds to fly three practice shows a day, in addition to their operational flying. Each pilot averaged over 20 hours a month and many landings and take-offs were involved. Sixty hours' flying meant 120 sorties. After every display practice there was an 'inquest' to sort out any inconsistencies; at these suggestions for possible improvements were

made, and cine-films run through. The adjutant, Flt Lt John Vickery, who also acted as the commentator during the actual displays, watched the show from the ground. All this meant that an accurate assessment of each performance could be attained, and every pilot found that he learned something new every time.

Before each show the CO briefed the nine pilots who were to fly in the formation and the programme was explained. In the air the nine aircraft (at this time the team had not yet worked up to thirteen aircraft – the writer flew in the leader's two-seater T.7) form up and listen out continually on the agreed R/T frequency for the leader's instructions. Only the leader talks, unless there is any particular need for a pilot to acknowledge an order, which is pre-arranged.

The leader calls: 'Flying down now for Diamond Nine loop. Relaxing back pressure.

The Blue Diamonds at Diyarbakir, Turkey, with Turkish Air Force RF-84s and Canberra WJ626, on 18 October 1961. The Blue Diamonds were en route to Tehran for a display at an air show on 20 October in honour of the Shah of Iran. (*Brian Allchin*)

'111 Squadron had as a regular show flown two teams – a nine- and a five-ship formation joining up at the end with the two airborne spares to fly a sixteen-aircraft loop to break for landing. Brian Mercer's "end plan" was to fly a sixteen-ship formation as a normal display, flying the formation in as tight a pattern as you could fly a Diamond nine. This had not been perfomed before. When the team were up to scratch Air Ministry photographer Mick Chase came out to Cyprus to take some publicity photos – a display was flown for RAF Akrotiri and then Nicosia, and the Blue Diamonds were in business. We headed back to the UK. In April the first displays were flown as a nine-ship for films and ITV – the first public show was the open day at RAF Wildenrath. Later, during May, three aircraft were added to make twelve, which started shows as three sections of four, which joined up during the first loop, later shed the three aircraft and finished as a nine.

'Finally, on 20 July 1961, the sixteen was first flown and thereafter this became the normal show. Starting as four sections of four aircraft the team joined up as sixteen during the final loop, did a full show as a sixteen then split into four fours to perform co-ordinated manoeuvres followed by opposition bomb bursts. The final event was a sixteen echelon run in for most of the subsequent shows.

'In October the team flew out to Cyprus and then on to Tehran to fly a display for the Shah of Iran on 20 October. On the way back to the UK, a display was put on for the Crown Prince of Greece at Athens. This ended the 1961 season and normal operational flying continued until March 1962.'

Flt Lt Tony Aldridge, pilot, Blue Diamonds

Looping – NOW!' 'NOW' is the key word for the beginning of a manoeuvre. In a formation change the word 'GO' indicates the start. Thus, 'T-bone – GO! Re-form Diamond Nine – GO! Smoke on – GO!' and then, at the completion of the manoeuvre, 'Smoke off – GO!'

The normal repertoire with nine aircraft followed a regular pattern, each manoeuvre being separated by a wing-over or a tight turn in front of the crowd: Diamond Nine loop; Diamond Nine roll, with smoke; T-bone loop, with smoke; Delta roll; Wine-glass loop (breaking 4 and 5); Half-Swan roll, with smoke; Line-abreast loop (breaking 6 and 7); Box-Five roll, with smoke; and Bomb-burst loop, with smoke. After re-forming into two echelons the Hunters came in and executed a double loop in echelon. The basic box-four formation readily lends itself to expansion, and while initially 92 Squadron's team consisted of nine aircraft it could easily be increased to twelve or sixteen aircraft, allowing in the latter four split formations of four aircraft each.

Flying in the pattern of a perfect diamond, the nine all-blue Hunter F.6 jet fighters approached the airfield at a steady 450mph, barely 4ft separating the aircraft. As one integrated whole they climbed in front of the spectators, their Rolls-Royce turbojets roaring out a deeper note, and the sun flashed on their undersides as they reached the inverted position. Coming out of the loop they rolled, again as one, and white smoke was emitted to leave billowing trails from the aircraft. The Hunters performed a precise wing-over and, following some fantastically precise manoeuvring on the part of the pilots, in the next second the formation had changed, now forming a 'T-bone', seven in line abreast with two forming the tail. The spectators at the display stood up for fear of missing anything of the intricate evolutions going on above them.

The smoke was cut off and dispersed. The aircraft went up in another loop, the smoke switched on again, and one looked carefully but in vain to detect any variation between the spacing of the aircraft. They flew a tight turn in front of the grandstand; re-formed again, this time into a 'delta' pattern. And so on. During the ten-minute show the crowd was treated to a fine exhibition of flying,

The Blue Diamonds (T.7 XL571, now painted blue, left) at Meherab in Iran on 20 October 1961 with French Air Force Dassault Mystère IVAs. That month 92 Squadron performed displays at Akrotiri, Nicosia and Episkopi in Cyprus, on 14, 16 and 17 October respectively, as well as one in front of the Crown Prince of Greece at Elefsis on 23 October. (*Brian Allchin*)

A Blue Diamonds F.6 breaks away from the formation during a photo sortie over England in 1961. (*Brian Allchin*)

A pair of Blue Diamonds Hunter F.6s over England with the Gloster Meteor T.7 camera ship. (*Brian Allchin*)

which included seven different formations. On the 'wine-glass' loop two aircraft left the formation; two more left on completion of the seven-aircraft line-abreast loop, and the remaining five formed up into a tight box, the rear aircraft flying just below the leader to avoid his slipstream. The five aircraft rolled, emitting smoke and went up for another loop. As they came out of it, heading directly for the airfield, they suddenly broke away, each flying off in a different direction at a height of 500ft, trailing smoke in a classic finale which had come to be known as a 'bomb-burst'.

The spectators, a little breathless from concentration, watched the Hunters as they came in to land, sometimes touching down on the runway in formations of three, sometimes making a stream landing one behind the other. They landed smoothly, without a bump, at around 145mph. A tiny puff of smoke from the friction of the rubber tyres touching the concrete and then the Hunters taxied past to the applause of the crowd. As they

moved away towards their dispersal base people could see the squadron markings of a red-and-yellow chequerboard on the nose of each aircraft, the badge of a striking cobra raising its head from between the squares, and the white bone-domes of the pilots in the blue Hunters, decked with white flash-lines and white wing-tips. The Blue Diamonds had finished their show for the day. Now the Hunter pilots could relax after the severe mental concentration and physical effort required for such accurate and close formation flying.

With the arrival of the Lightning F.2 in 19 and 92 Squadrons in late 1962/early 1963, the Hunter F.6 was phased out of Fighter Command and 1962 was 92 Squadron's second and last season as a Hunter display team. Perhaps because it was the Hunter's last chance to go out in a blaze of glory, the air-to-air gunnery team that year made an extra special effort to win it for the RAF. In June the RAF won the NATO AIRCENT gun-firing competition for the first time, using Hunter F.6s with their

Flg Off Brian Allchin in front of F.6 XG186 'J-Juliet' of 92 Squadron, the Blue Diamonds. This Hunter flew for the first time on 2 September 1956 and first served with 19 and 66 Squadrons. It later served with DFLS and was purchased by Hawker Siddeley Aircraft on 6 October 1967. (*Brian Allchin*)

30mm cannon. Traditionally, RCAF Sabres using .5-inch machine-guns had won this competition in the past. At Leconfield, 92 Squadron (using Blue Diamonds' aircraft) hosted the 1962 RAF team and after a shoot-off the four team-members were selected. They were Blue Diamonds pilots Sqn Ldr Mercer (leader) and Flt Lt Tony Aldridge, along with Flt Lt Pete Highton

Diamonds with 12 Aces

'Sqn Ldr Mercer explained to me how 92 Squadron had built up its present international display standard. "Last year 92 were the reserve to back up 111 Squadron. They did a few displays, then at the end of last year 111 re-equipped with Lightnings and, as 92 had been the reserve team, it seemed logical they should take over the commitment. I took command in October last year, and the more inexperienced pilots were transferred to other fighter squadrons because we needed experienced men. After the Christmas break we went out to Cyprus for two months to train. When we came back we put on a display for the C-in-C of Fighter Command. We passed muster – and we were in business."

'Mercer, together with four of his other pilots, has previous experience of aerobatic flying with 111 Squadron. "After four acrobatic sorties you feel a sense of exhilaration but you feel like a pint and a cigarette as well. We're operating with 12 aircraft now. Something no one has done before. This is a job which demands 100 per cent mental and physical concentration. The concentration required is so much that although you are only up for 30 minutes, three sorties a day is enough for anybody. The physical strain? Well, we reach a maximum of 4G. In normal fighter flying you can go across 7G. You get a sense of satisfaction out of it – but it's bloody hard work, it takes a hell of a lot of effort."

'One might suppose that ace pilots have to follow a spartan regime in the same way as top athletes. "Not really," Sqn Ldr Mercer told me. "But the night before a display the rule is no late parties. And I insist on them having eight hours' sleep. Well, I don't have to insist; they know it without my telling them. But you don't have to be a tremendous physical specimen to be an aerobatic pilot. I don't have them all out for PT in the morning – mainly because I'd have to do it myself! You don't have to do 100 yards in 10 seconds. But you have to do it in 13. Most of them play games – squash, for example, is very popular . . . By the time a chap reaches 36 or 37 it gets a bit too much for him. You've got to have dead-cool nerves. But the most important thing for a formation aerobatic pilot is that you've got to like it."

'"Your air discipline must be absolutely tight. There's no room for the individualist. The Household Cavalry and the Guards aren't in it. If you're more than 2ft out of position it shows. And your aircraft may be only 4ft away from the next chap's. But I wouldn't say it was a dangerous existence. 111 Squadron's accident record was the best in Fighter Command. When you have to concentrate so hard you're far less likely to be careless . . . All the pilots in this squadron have to be very experienced. They're all volunteers and they've all had at least one previous tour in a fighter squadron. They must all be experts at handling their aircraft – we can't afford to have anyone who is barely average . . . We have an aerobatic squadron first to show the flag, second to give the RAF publicity, and third as an incentive to recruiting. The three are interlinked really. But I should emphasise that it doesn't cost the country any more money to keep us going. The RAF couldn't afford a full-time aerobatic team as the Americans do – they've got three in fact. We're a normal fighter squadron, and we have a full training commitment. During the summer we can't do so much operational flying, but this is more than counter-balanced by the experience level of the pilots."

'It was certainly refreshing to find sixteen young men who really are happy in their work. And to meet them made one realize that anybody who says the sense of adventure, the zest for living, has disappeared from British youth is talking through his hat. For every one of those Blue Diamonds, there must be hundreds more pilots who would give their bottom dollar to be strapped in the ejection seats of those Hunters.'

Philip Ray, 'Diamonds with 12 Aces', Men Only, November 1961

The Blue Diamonds in line abreast formation. (*Brian Allchin*)

Around October 1967 Brian Allchin was driving along in his car when he passed a RAF Queen Mary transporter in a lay-by with a Hunter fuselage under tarpaulins. He pulled over to investigate and was amazed to discover that the Hunter was none other than 'J-Juliet', now destined for conversion to Hunter 56A for the Indian Air Force! IAF A941 was delivered to India on 22 March 1969. (*Brian Allchin*)

XF449, one of a single production batch of a hundred F.6s built by Armstrong Whitworth and retrospectively fitted with wing leading-edge extensions and gun blast deflectors. This aircraft served with 263 and 19 Squadrons before joining the Blue Diamonds as 'S'. It was written off on 18 October 1963. (via *Frank Mason*)

of 2nd TAF and Flt Lt Piet van Wyk of 19 Squadron. The RAF victory was quite remarkable as the .5-inch machine-gun was much easier to harmonize and the Sabre was a very stable gun platform. The Hunter was a livelier aircraft and the 30mm cannon was 'quite a handful'. Tony Aldridge adds:

> After the NATO AIRCENT competition it was straight back to aerobatics full time, and apart from a few nine-ship displays the main aim was the sixteen-ship display at the SBAC show in September. This was done with the aircraft operating from Farnborough itself. After Farnborough, there were practices for the Battle of Britain day and three shows on the day. Then in October 1962, there were a few practices for the Blue Diamonds' final show, which was at Middleton St George on 13 October. And that was it for the Blue Diamonds aerobatic team. In 1963, the squadron reverted to normal operational flying and converted to English Electric Lightnings the following

year. We took part in the 1964 SBAC show with Lightnings doing a stream reheat and rotation take-off from Farnborough led by Brian Mercer with some of the Blue Diamond pilots still on the squadron.

For the 1963 season the Firebirds of 56 (Lightning) Squadron were selected as the official RAF aerobatic team. The Yellowjacks from 4 FTS performed at Farnborough in 1964. That same year the CFS's Red Pelicans team, flying six Jet Provost T4s, took the national stage. Then in May 1965 the Red Arrows performed in public for the first time and in 1969 they were established on a permanent basis within the CFS as a squadron in their own right. As good as these teams undoubtedly are, the Blue Diamonds' unique sixteen aeros display, crafted and perfected by Brian Mercer, will never be repeated.

CHAPTER 6

HOME THOUGHTS FROM ABROAD

What the RAF needs is a sophisticated aircraft with tactical flexibility in order to fulfil our obligations abroad.

House of Commons, 1967

A dramatic career change, begun in 1958, saw the Hunter success story enter one of its most impressive chapters. Hawkers had long been aware of its potential as a very successful ground-attack aircraft, and the RAF now needed a new aircraft to replace the de Havilland Venom FB.4 in this role in the Middle East. Front runners, though, were the Hunting-Percival Jet Provost, and the Folland Gnat. Both were RAF trainers and therefore cheaper options for conversion. The Gnat and Jet Provost were sent to Aden to be used in trials flown by pilots from the Central Fighting Establishment's Air Fighting Development Squadron (AFDS). (In August 1959 the AFDS and the AWDS amalgamated, and the enhanced AFDS moved to RAF Coltishall in Norfolk at the end of the month.) Although the Hunter was considered in some circles to be uneconomical for conversion to ground-attack, two F.6s, equipped with tail parachutes (courtesy of experience gained with Swiss Hunters), were allowed to take part in the trials. Two Hunter F.6s, XK150 and XK151, the last production single-seater fighter variants delivered to the RAF, were drawn from No. 5 MU and flown out to RAF Khormaksar, Aden. There they joined Jet Provost T.3 XN117, and a production Indian Air Force Folland Gnat F.1 IE1064 (temporarily serialled XN122) in the Venom Replacement Evaluation Trials (VRET). The two Hunters completely outclassed the two training types in the 'hot and high' conditions.

On 15 May 1959 Hawkers decided to build a company-owned and sponsored demonstration two-seat aircraft by reusing major components from damaged and derelict Hunters. IF-19, a Belgian Mk 6 that had suffered a serious landing accident after only 24 flying hours, became the basis of the new aircraft. Its undamaged centre and rear fuselage with tailplane and elevators were used together with an Avon 203 engine and gearbox from AWA-built F.6 XF378, the wings, fin and rudder from Belgian F.6 IF-67, and a two-seat Indian Mk 66 nose used as a ground display unit for the 1959 Paris Air Show. G-APUX ('Gappucks', as it became known), was first flown on 12 August 1959 by Bill Bedford, who used this aircraft to perform his unique inverted spinning demonstrations, trailing smoke for display purposes, at Farnborough in 1959 and 1960. 'Gappucks' was painted in military livery and from May 1963 to 1965, was used for training purposes in Iraq, Lebanon and Jordan. In 1967 G-APUX was refurbished and acquired by Chile as a T.72, being delivered as J-718 on 9 August. It is now a static exhibit at the Chile National Aviation Museum. (*HAL* via *Frank Mason*)

XE535 was built as an F.6 at Kingston and was first flown on 17 January 1956. It served with 20 and 26 Squadrons before being returned to Hawker Siddeley Aircraft on 2 February 1961 for conversion to FGA.9 standard. It was subsequently issued to 28 Squadron but was lost in a crash on 28 December 1962. (*HSA* via *Frank Mason*)

The F.6s of 92 Squadron at Hal Far, Malta, in 1960. Valletta is in the background. (*Brian Allchin*)

No. 92 Squadron ground personnel pose for the camera in front of F.6 XF521/RD during the Hal Far detachment in 1960. XF521 was flown by Sqn Ldr R.H.B. Dixon, the CO from October 1958 to October 1960. On 6 September 1967 XF521 was purchased by Hawker Siddeley Aircraft for conversion to Indian Hunter 56A (A938), being delivered on 22 March 1969. In 1960, 92 Squadron's Falcons were Fighter Command's reserve aerobatic team and flew five aircraft at several displays during the year. (*Brian Allchin*)

Dawn alert for a 92 Squadron F.6 pilot during a detachment at Duxford one cold November day in 1960. (*Brian Allchin*)

In 1958, a conversion contract to modify forty Hunter F.6s withdrawn from MUs to full FGA.9 standard was placed with Hawker Siddeley. This was followed, in 1959, by a second conversion contract, undertaken by the RAF and company

'In 1958 the MoD carried out a study to determine the RAF's new ground-attack aircraft. In the final group were Hunters, Gnats and Jet Provosts. Before the Hunters went to the Middle East for their part in the trials we sent a party to West Raynham to fit XK150 and 151 with new ailerons with a honeycomb internal structure. Subsequently, the Hunters won the contest with the result that the FGA.9 was born. Although the ailerons fitted were satisfactory, they were not regarded as essential and were not specified on the Mk 9.'

Eric Hayward

working party at Horsham St Faith, to bring thirty-six F.6s up to Interim FGA.9 standard. Between 1960 and 1965, four more contracts were awarded to convert a further fifty-two F.6s to FGA.9 standard. All were fitted with a tail parachute, increased cockpit ventilation and refrigeration, increased pilot's oxygen supply, and provision for carrying 230-gallon drop-tanks.

In addition to the Hunter's standard four-gun armament, strengthened wings enabled the FGA.9 to carry a wide variety of external stores. The two inboard pylons could carry 500lb or 1,000lb bombs, a cluster of six 3-inch rocket projectiles, a honeycomb battery containing twenty-four or thirty-seven 2-inch folding-fin rockets, or a carrier holding two 25lb practice bombs. Removal of the outboard pylons permitted the carrying of four

Mk 12 rocket rails, each fitted with three or four 3-inch rocket projectiles with 60lb warheads. (In 1967 the 68mm SNEB rocket, which comprised eighteen rockets in a pod, was fitted to the Hunter's outboard wing pylon to replace the '3-inch drainpipe' rocket, which dated back to the Second World War.) It brought the Hunter's all-up weight to more than 25,000lb, a remarkable achievement given the hot and high environment in which the FGA.9 was to operate.

The first FGA.9, XG135, flew on 3 July 1959, powered by a non-surge Avon 207. (XG135 was lost on 6 April 1973 when Flt Lt G. McLeod of 45 Squadron abandoned the aircraft on finals when he received a fire warning. He ejected safely, the Hunter crashing 2 miles east of Wittering.) Initially, the converted aircraft retained their original Avon 203 engines but later most were progressively re-engined with the Avon 207. Fitted with long-range, 230-gallon drop

FGA.9 'C' of 8 Squadron, flown by Flt Lt D.G. Hazell, showing the unit's distinctive gambiyah emblem, which was used as part of the crest of 8 Squadron and was incorporated in the badge of the APL (Aden Protectorate Levies). The gambiyah is a treasured weapon and a most decorative example of craftsmanship. (*Colin Smith*)

The Straw that Broke the Camel's Back

'I arrived at RAF Khormaksar, Aden, in February 1960, the same time as 8 Squadron re-equipped with the Hunter. These replaced Venoms. The aircraft were mainly Mk 9s plus two Mk 7 trainers, and three Mk 10s for photo-reconnaissance. I worked in the Hunter central armoury, which served 8, and later 208, Squadron, which arrived in 1961 from Eastleigh, Kenya. The central armoury was responsible for cannons, ejection seats and rocket launchers. In addition, part of my duty was crash recovery. During the two-year period we lost about five aircraft. In all cases the pilots were killed. One crash, which involved FR.10 XE579 [on 8 August 1961 near Zinjibah, Eastern Aden Protectorate], occurred about 20 miles up country from RAF Khormaksar. The pilot, Flg Off E.J. 'John' Volkers was killed. The terrain was such we had to use camels to salvage the aircraft. Hunters were used to good effect in the Radfan against dissident tribesman. On odd occasions they came back to base with holes from old muzzle-loading flintlocks, which were mounted on the horn of a camel's saddle and fired ball ammunition.'

Eighteen-year-old Richard D. Rix, RAF armourer, 8 and 208 Squadrons, Aden, 1960–2

Last one coming up! Fred (on the right) and Larry load the first of six concrete-headed practice rockets to a No. 8 Squadron FGA.9 at RAF Khormaksar, summer 1963. This was their last job before returning to the UK (tour-ex). Note the appropriately placed mug of tea, yes tea; even hot beverages were welcome in the torrid heat of Aden. (*Ray Deacon*)

tanks on the inner pylons and 100-gallon tanks on the outer pylons, the first FGA.9s for 8 Squadron arrived at Khormaksar during mid-January 1960 and a full complement of twelve Hunters was on strength by the beginning of February. (The first Hunters for the Middle East were two T.7s, XL613 and XL615, which arrived on 22 September 1959.) Later, units overseas took priority when it came to re-equipping with the FGA.9 and in March 1960 208 Squadron began receiving FGA.9s.

In June 1960 208 Squadron flew to Nairobi in Kenya and began operating from Eastleigh. On 25 June the Iraqi prime minister, General Abdul Karim Kassim, announced that neighbouring Kuwait was an integral part of his country. Under an existing agreement Britain prepared to send

military assistance to the small Arab kingdom, anticipating that Iraq would attack Kuwait on or around 14 July (Iraq's National Day). On 30 June 1961, as part of the military build-up, plans were made to move the FGA.9s of both 8 Squadron (based at Khormaksar) and 208 Squadron (Embakasi in Kenya) to Bahrain to meet the expected threat. Ironically, Iraq at this time also included two squadrons of Hunter F.6s in its inventory. On 1 July, 8 Squadron's Hunters landed at Kuwait's new airport, to be joined the following day by the FGA.9s of 208 Squadron. However, the Iraqi threat to Kuwait did not materialize. No. 8 Squadron remained in the kingdom a while longer before returning to Khormaksar, but 208 Squadron returned to Bahrain.

'In the early 1960s most RAF personnel posted to the Middle and Far East were flown out in military or chartered civilian Britannias, but a few unfortunates suffered the experience of "cruising" out there in one of HM's troop ships, HMS *Nevasa* in my case. At the time of my arrival, there were two Hunter units, 8 Squadron operating fourteen FGA.9s, four FR.10s and two T.7s, and 208 Squadron with twelve FGA.9s and a T.7. As a quick reaction force of eight FGA.9s had to be stationed at RAF Muharraq in Bahrain for relocation to Kuwait in the event of an Iraqi threat to the tiny state, each squadron was tasked with supplying a detachment of requisite aircraft and crews on a two-month rotation. This continued until March 1963.

'With terrorist attacks on British Army convoys and tribal in-fighting in the Aden Protectorate increasing, 43 Squadron was transferred from Cyprus to Khormaksar in March 1963, bringing with it twelve FGA.9s and a T.7 to bolster the RAF's ground-attack capability. At the same time 1417 Flight was re-formed by transferring the four FR.10s and two T.7s from 8 Squadron and a T.7 each from the other two units. It was tasked with providing photo-recce and training support for the three squadrons. Following the arrival of 43 Squadron, the two-month detachments to Bahrain occurred every four months. The situation had remained unchanged for little more than a year when 208 Squadron was transferred to Bahrain on a permanent basis, and 8 and 43 Squadrons and 1417 Flight was formed into the Hunter Strike Wing, which included 37 Squadron with its Shackleton MR.2s.'

SAC Ray Deacon, air wireless mechanic, 8 Squadron, RAF Khormaksar, Aden, April 1962–April 1964

30-mm Aden cannon shells for air-to-ground practice gun-firing by Hunter FGA.9s on the range near RAF Khormaksar, 1961. The colours on the 30-mm ammo heads denoted the type of High Explosive/live ammo it was. Once out of their particular ammo boxes there was no easy way of telling whether rounds were HE, Incendiary, Armour Piercing (used against armoured vehicles), SAP/HE (Semi Armour Piercing/High Explosive). Therefore, the 30-mm shells had pre-arranged, colour-coded tips – red, green, yellow, blue and brown. For air-to-ground practice 'Ball' was used. At the start of a practice all four guns would be loaded with fifty rounds, but as scores were out of a hundred only two guns were used, and the fuses were removed from the other two guns. The fuses were replaced after landing so that the next pilot used this pair of guns. Then the gun pack would be reloaded. When all the hessian targets had been 'engaged', a lull was called while the holes were counted and then colour marked (with a long pole dipped in paint) before the next wave. Air-to-air gun-firing was not practised in Aden (there were no Meteor 8 target tugs – cine practice was assessed using the portable GGSR (Gyro Gun Sight Recording) camera, which was clipped on top of the gun sight for training flights. (*Colin Smith*)

FGA.9s of 8 Squadron on the line at Khormaksar in 1961. Behind is a Blackburn Beverley of 84 Squadron. Beverleys were used to supply the Army's up-country posts and to fly the routes up to the Persian Gulf and as far south as Salisbury, Rhodesia, in Hunter support and mobility exercises in the Protectorate and Kenya. (*Colin Smith*)

FGA.9 XF455/T of 8 Squadron taxies past at RAF Khormaksar, Aden, late in 1961. This Baginton-built F.6 first served with 247 and 43 Squadrons. After conversion it was flown for the first time as a FGA.9 on 7 November 1959 by Bill Bedford, being delivered on 3 December 1959. After serving in 8 Squadron in the Middle East XF455 passed to 20 Squadron in the Far East, and on 19 September 1964 it crashed into the sea off Singapore, killing the pilot. (*Colin Smith*)

As Kenya was to gain independence from Britain, 208 Squadron moved to Aden during November 1962 where more trouble was brewing. President Abdul Nasser of Egypt attempted to remove the British from Aden using Egyptian armed insurgents in the neighbouring state of Yemen. A mountainous area known as the Radfan, 20 miles long by 15 miles wide, 35 miles north of Aden, was the main stronghold of the Yemeni-backed insurgents. No. 208 Squadron's Hunter FGA.9s and a few Shackletons carried out leaflet-dropping missions, followed by bombing strikes against the insurgents in the Radfan. On 1 March 1963, 43 Squadron, which had converted to the FGA.9

at Leuchars before moving to Cyprus in June 1961, moved to Khormaksar. Tension in Aden reached a new peak on 10 December 1963 when Yemeni insurgents threw a hand grenade at a group of dignitaries at the Khormaksar civil airport as they were bidding farewell to the departing High Commissioner, Sir Kennedy Trevaskis. His assistant, George Henderson, pushed Sir Kennedy aside but Henderson was killed when the grenade exploded. At this time 43 Squadron was the only FGA.9 squadron at Khormaksar (1417 Flight, part of the Tactical Wing at Khormaksar, operated FR.10 Hunters), as 8 Squadron's Hunters were at Bahrain and 208 Squadron was temporarily detached to Nairobi.

XF436/U, photographed outside the 8 Squadron hangar in October 1962, was one of four FR.10s operated by 8 Squadron from April 1961 until March 1963, when they were transferred, together with four T.7s from the Aden squadrons, to the re-formed 1417 Flight, also based at Khormaksar. (*Ray Deacon*)

Between flights, the Hunters had to be turned round, fully re-armed and fuelled-up in 20 minutes, so good teamwork was essential. Undoubtedly the hardest job on the line was changing the 30mm Aden gun-pack, a task that required three armourers and the assistance of a trusted Arab worker. In this view, taken at Khormaksar in mid-1963, 'Jock' Harmon (right) works with two of his colleagues to lower a pack on an 8 Squadron FGA.9, while the Arab collects the cannon links. As a safety precaution, the Mk 9 and Mk 10 Hunters were fitted with a special plug under the port mainplane which, when disconnected, prevented the guns and rockets being accidentally fired on the ground. It was the job of one of the armourers to connect the plug on each aircraft as it reached the perimeter track and unplug them on their return. (*Ray Deacon*)

Ray Byatt marshalling 8 Squadron FGA.9 XE618 at Khormaksar in early 1963. Every ground engineer on any squadron was trained to marshal aircraft and was responsible for any mishaps to an aircraft under his control. Concentration was vital, especially so when the aircraft were armed with cannon and rocket rounds. The pilot is probably Bill Shepherd as he always wore a distinctive coloured bone-dome. The rocket rails, 230-gallon drop-tanks, lack of gun blast deflectors and brake-chute housing distinguished the FGA.9 from the F.6, from which every FGA.9 was converted. Internal enhancements included additional oxygen for the longer flight duration, 'air conditioning' and an Avon 207 series engine in place of the 203. Note the blue trolley which is positioned ready to remove the empty gun-pack. (*Ray Deacon*)

From July 1961 to March 1963, 8 Squadron alternated with 208 Squadron on detachments to Bahrain on a two-monthly cycle. When 43 Squadron moved from Cyprus to Aden in 1963 the detachments occurred every four months. During the two-month stint at Bahrain the units often deployed to Sharjah for two weeks where they could practise gun and rocket firing on the Jeb-a-Jib range. Here FGA.9 XG255, with Bill Shepherd at the controls, comes into land at Sharjah after a summer 1963 sortie on the Jeb-a-Jib range, as seen by the soot-covered gun-ports. A new nose-wheel door and borrowed nose-cone are indications that the aircraft had recently sustained minor damage. XG255 became Jordanian FGA.73 (825) in December 1967. (*Ray Deacon*)

As the Hunter had a pressurized fuel system, fuel spillage was a rare occurrence but it had to be tackled swiftly in the Aden heat to avoid an explosive incident. Here, at Khormaksar in early 1963, airfield fire crews lay a blanket of foam while the Air Sea Rescue Sycamore helicopter hovers nearby in case it is needed. In the foreground is 8 Squadron's FGA.9 XE609/A, with two 1417 Flight FR.10s behind, XE614/PL and XF441/JD. XE614 was purchased by Hawker Siddeley Aviation in June 1971 and converted to a FR.74B, being delivered on 21 February 1973 to 141 'Merlin' Squadron of the Singaporean Air Force. (*Ray Deacon*)

It was usual practice for the Hunters to take off in pairs but on rare occasions, such as practice formation sorties, a trio might take off together. Here, three 8 Squadron FGA.9s depart Bahrain in mid-1963. (*Ray Deacon*)

No. 8 Squadron's FGA.9 XE618, piloted by Chris Cureton, is given the all clear at Khormaksar in the autumn of 1963. XE618 (and XF421) received lower waistlines during refurbishment by 5 MU at RAF Kemble in 1962, but this was not continued. (*Ray Deacon*)

The Plastic Flower Mob

'The Hunter squadrons in Aden became known by wags everywhere as "The Plastic Flower Mob". Why? "There were many funerals and no flowers grow there!"'

During the early months of 1964 an increased number of hit-and-run raids by Yemeni aircraft on villages close to the Aden border culminated in an attack by an armed helicopter and two MiG fighters on Bulaq, close to Beihan. The village and a frontier guard post in the district were bombed and strafed with machine-gun fire, as were camels, other livestock and tents nearby. In retaliation, the RAF was ordered to attack Yemeni insurgents who had gained control of a fort at Harib a few miles into Yemeni territory near Beihan. The Hunters dropped leaflets to warn the civilian population before beginning their attack on 28 March.

'In a combined operation with four FGA.9s from 43 Squadron and one FR.10 from 1417 Flight, five 8 Squadron FGA.9s were utilized on an attack on a Yemeni Fort called Harib on 28 March. The FR.10 and one 8 Squadron FGA.9 (XG237: Flg Off S. Bottom) took off at 0830 to drop warning leaflets over the target, giving the occupants 15 minutes to vacate the place. These two then provided top-cover for the main force of eight FGA.9s (XF440: Wg Cdr J. Jennings; XG256: Flt Lt Humphreyson; XE609: Flt Lt G. Williams; XE620: Flt Lt M. Johnson) as it carried out the attack with cannon and HE rockets. The solidly built stone fort, which was located a few miles inside the Yemen, was almost completely destroyed.'

PRO F540: Records for 8 Squadron – 28 March 1964

Sqn Ldr Phil Champniss was the commanding officer of 43 Squadron at the time of the attack on Fort Harib on 28 March 1964. He describes the events 'from the hot seat':

XL613/Z, one of two T.7s operated by 8 Squadron (the other was XL565), starting up in 1963 at Bahrain prior to departing on the 1,300-mile flight to Khormaksar at the conclusion of a two-month detachment. (*Ray Deacon*)

The Hunter pan at Khormaksar could hold twenty aircraft and was shared by three units at any one time: 1417 Flight plus two from 8, 43 and 208 Squadrons. By contrast the pan at Bahrain could only hold ten Hunters but as the usual detachment comprised only eight FGA.9s and a T.7 the far end was used by two 13 Squadron Canberra PR.9s on detachment from Cyprus. This summer 1963 view includes FGA.9s XF376, XE651, XE654, XF421, XE620/F and XG255. XE620/F was flown by the 8 Squadron CO, Sqn Ldr Rex Knight, on the 1961 goodwill visit to the Royal Rhodesian Air Force base at Gwelo, Southern Rhodesia. XE620 was a Kingston-built F.6 aircraft, flown for the first time on 12 June 1956 by Frank Bullen and delivered to 111 Squadron on 4 July that year. It later served with 263 Squadron. Returned to Hawkers in 1959 and converted to FGA.9, XE620 later served with 43 Squadron at Khormaksar, and in April 1968 was purchased by HSA and converted to Indian Hunter Mk 56A (A967), being delivered on 31 July 1969. (*Ray Deacon*)

I had twenty-four operational pilots, although at one stage we actually dropped down to ten. (This became a very critical factor later when the Radfan 'thing' started.) We spent hour upon hour doing continuous air patrols over the Beihan border, which for sheer boredom has got the Nobel prize because you are just bowling around in circles pretending to look terribly operational. Of course you couldn't go too fast, otherwise you hadn't got enough fuel to do it and come back again, so we were bumping about at rather slow speeds at about 6,000ft so you actually weren't galloping through fuel too much. Beihan was an area quite a long way north-east of Aden in the hills on the Yemeni border. It was just Aden and Yemen. There was none of this 'North' and 'South' Yemen business. I never saw a single aircraft from the other side although the army on the ground kept on reporting every time I just left, 'Oh gosh, here's one coming across,' and to this day I don't know if they were just being humorous or whether they actually saw anything. I think there was an indication, but certainly none of my guys ever saw it, and it was a bit boring. We in fact used to fly with 2 x 230s and 2 x 100 gallon [drop-tanks] on the outboard pylons, so we were heavy and cumbersome, but the rule was that you threw off the 100s if you got bounced. In fact they were empty by the time you got there because you used to feed out

as inners and then [use] the internal fuel. Incidentally, of course you couldn't fly the big tanks and the outboard tanks if you had rockets on because they took up the under store carrier.

An event which got quite a lot of press coverage at the time, but you don't often see it mentioned these days when you read the history of the Hunter, was the Beihan Fort business. The sheriff of Beihan was on our side. i.e. he liked the Brits; [he] was getting a bit of hassle, and so it was decided politically that as a sort of 'finger wagging' bit, we'd knock down the fort. It was quite large and old, not very well built and it would fall over fairly easily.

We took eight aircraft up there. Wg Cdr John Jennings, OC Strike Wing at the time, led the first four, from 8 Squadron, and I led the back four of 43 Squadron. We used 3-inch rockets and these went down quite successfully. We took 48 each – 3 rows of 16 – and we fired them off in salvoes. That was 16 at a go. The post-strike photographs taken by 1417 Flight with their FR.10s indicated that it had been very effective.

SAC Ray Deacon, an air wireless mechanic with 8 Squadron recalls events on the ground on the day of the attack:

The Avon 207 starting cycle was initiated using an AVPIN liquid starter, which burnt for several seconds. The system was usually reliable but on occasions the engine would fail to light up, leaving a pool of fuel in the jet-pipe. After a short wait the sequence was tried again and flames would shoot out from the jet pipe. Known as a wet start, one such instance is depicted in this view of an 8 Squadron FGA.9 at Khormaksar in early 1964. (*Ray Deacon*)

No. 8 Squadron FGA.9 XE609/A on the pan at Khormaksar, summer 1963. XE609 served with
No. 208 Squadron before being written offf on 7 April 1966. (*Ray Deacon*)

Following a wheels-up landing at Bahrain, the front half of 43 Squadron's FGA.9 XJ684 was mated to
the rear section of a grounded 8 Squadron machine while repairs were carried out on the damaged
sections. The tail fin and nose-cone were borrowed from a 208 Squadron aircraft. XJ684 is seen
here taxiing out for the long flight to Khormaksar bearing the colours of both units in December 1963.
With the formation of the Hunter Wing in 1964, the colours of 8 and 43 Squadrons were applied on
either side of the roundel. (*Ray Deacon*)

A 'lo' pair of 8 Squadron FGA.9s, XF376 and XG154, taking off from Khormaksar, early in 1964. On four-ship sorties, the first pair would normally climb steeply away from the runway (hi) to enable the second pair to keep low (lo) and build up speed for a swift join-up. In RAF jargon this was known as 'hi-lo.' (*Ray Deacon*)

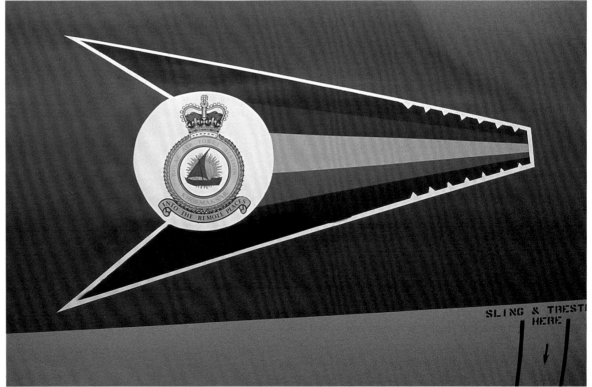

Following the re-forming of 1417 Flight in March 1963 a new unit pennant was produced by the Hunter Wing's aircraft finisher, Peter Richards, and was applied to the forward fuselage of the unit's FR.10s and later to the T.7s. (*Ray Deacon*)

At 03:30 on the morning of the 28th, we were rudely woken by the dulcet tones of the duty sergeant, ordering us to report to Squadron HQ immediately. No shaving, no washing, just get dressed and board the transport waiting outside. Fortunately, the sobriety of the previous evening meant that hangovers were few and apart from lack of sleep most of us had clear heads. As we were driven away, the realization quickly sank in that we had never been called out in the middle of the night before, so something rather special must be in the offing. On arrival at the pan, several pilots could be seen talking to each other as they moved between the various offices. No explanation was given to us groundcrew, however, until 'Chiefy' called us together and told us to prepare seven FGA.9s, two in reserve, and two 1417 Flight FR.10s, one in reserve, for an important operation. No. 43 Squadron personnel had also been called in to prepare five FGA.9s (one as reserve) for this joint operation.

Once the pre-flight checks were completed, those of us that were free assisted the riggers and armourers to replace the outer drop-tank pylons with additional rocket rails, a lengthy and fiddly task on the poorly lit pan. An hour or so later the rocket trolleys were towed along the back of the line, and while some helped with the mounting and connection of these high-explosive projectiles, others stuffed warning leaflets between the wings and flaps of the Mk 10s and two Mk 9s.

At this stage, an outline of the tactics employed on the heavier air-to-ground strikes by the Aden Hunter Wing may be useful. Two Hunters would depart some 15 minutes ahead of a main force and, while flying fast and low over the target, lower their flaps to release warning leaflets on to the target. The lead aircraft of the pair was usually an FGA.9 and this would be closely followed by an FR.10 taking photographs of the leaflets being dropped. By the time the inhabitants below read the instructions, they would have had 13 or so minutes to vacate the area or face certain oblivion. The main force, consisting of from four to eight FGA.9s, would then carry out the attack with 30mm HE cannon and rocket fire, while the leaflet-carrying aircraft maintained top cover. Once the attack was over, the FR.10 would make a final sweep to photograph the damage inflicted on the target.

As dawn began to break on the 28th, the first two pilots walked out to the line hut and signed the Form 700s for their particular aircraft, one FR.10 and one FGA.9, both fitted with HE gun-packs but no rockets. Once strapped in, they started up and taxied out for take-off. I was assigned to start one of the eight main force FGA.9s, this particular aircraft being flown by a young-looking Flt Lt Martin Johnson. He was very excited and eager to complete his pre-flight checks, almost running up the ladder and jumping into the cockpit. I handed him his parachute and seat straps, waited until he was safely belted in, removed the ejection seat safety pin and stowed it away before removing the ladder.

At a given signal from Wg Cdr Jennings in the lead aircraft, eight pilots hit their starting tits and seven AVPIN starters burst into life, their Avons lighting up within a few seconds. Why only seven? Sod's law! The starter failed on my aircraft. After applying a couple of hefty thumps on the starter panel relay boxes with the handle of my trusty screwdriver in the vain hope it might fire at the second attempt, I gave the signal to try once more, but again the starter failed. In an instant, the straps flew over Martin's shoulders and he was standing on the seat ready for the ladder to be re-attached. He climbed out and quickly ran to a spare aircraft, with me in hot pursuit. As he clambered in, the other Hunters began to taxi out and between the two of us, he was belted-up in record time.

Safety pin out, ladder away, a twirl of the forefinger and a welcoming blast from the AVPIN starter, closely followed by the healthy roar of the Avon. It could hardly have reached idling speed before he throttled it up and sped out on to the taxiway. By this time the others were accelerating down the Khormaksar runway on their take-off runs, while he must have reached a similar speed on his way to the threshold. Round the corner and on to the runway with Avon seemingly at full power throughout, then off he went in pursuit of the rest who were disappearing into the distant haze. Did he catch them? Of course he did, and the attack was executed precisely as planned. Photographs taken by the FR.10 before and after the raid revealed that the stone-built fort was virtually destroyed, as were an anti-aircraft gun and a number of vehicles. So good were the photographs that the warning leaflets could be clearly seen lying in and around the fort. And the attack had the desired effect: incursions by Yemeni aircraft ceased thereafter.

The attack by the Hunters was followed under cover of darkness by a paradrop by 22 SAS who prepared a drop zone for further reinforcements. At daybreak on the 29th the SAS came under

Due to the extreme heat encountered in Aden, the gases remaining in the AVPIN starter exhaust chamber at the end of the start cycle would often ignite and it was the responsibility of the groundcrew to prevent flames entering the starter panel bay. In this view Pete Wotton uses an asbestos glove to beat out the flames before latching the starter panel shut with the screwdriver. (*Ray Deacon*)

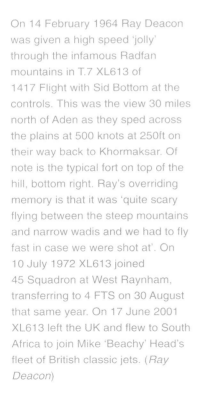

On 14 February 1964 Ray Deacon was given a high speed 'jolly' through the infamous Radfan mountains in T.7 XL613 of 1417 Flight with Sid Bottom at the controls. This was the view 30 miles north of Aden as they sped across the plains at 500 knots at 250ft on their way back to Khormaksar. Of note is the typical fort on top of the hill, bottom right. Ray's overriding memory is that it was 'quite scary flying between the steep mountains and narrow wadis and we had to fly fast in case we were shot at'. On 10 July 1972 XL613 joined 45 Squadron at West Raynham, transferring to 4 FTS on 30 August that same year. On 17 June 2001 XL613 left the UK and flew to South Africa to join Mike 'Beachy' Head's fleet of British classic jets. (*Ray Deacon*)

A pair of 8 Squadron FGA.9s swoop low over a splash-target during trials of new Kodak colour film in the gun cameras in the Gulf of Aden in March 1964. The wooden target was towed at high speed by the locally based RAF Air/Sea Rescue launch. (*Ray Deacon*)

Previous page, above: FGA.9 XK151 of 208 Squadron on the Khormaksar pan, March 1964. This was the last single-seater Hunter delivered to the RAF in 1957 and was one of two (XK150 being the other) to participate in the Middle East Venom replacement trials in Aden in 1958. XK151 was a Kingston-built F.6, which was flown for the first time on 16 June 1957 by Duncan Simpson and was delivered to the RAF in September that year. Converted to FGA.9 in 1959 and delivered to B Squadron early in 1960, it joined 45 Squadron at RAF Wittering on 4 June 1973, moving to the Hunter Wing via 71 MU on 28 January 1976. With the disbandment of 45 Squadron, XK151 joined the TWU in October 1976 and in 1978 transferred to Lossiemouth with 2 TWU. (*Ray Deacon*)

heavy fire while moving in to clear the Aden–Dhala road. Before long, they were surrounded by three times the expected numbers of enemy tribesmen – actually a disciplined force armed with mortars and machine-guns. Between them, 43 and 208 Squadrons flew eighteen sorties, firing 127 3-inch rockets and over 7,000 rounds of 30mm cannon. The battle raged for 30 hours and two British troopers were killed. Thereafter British ground forces supported by the FGA.9s harried and hunted down the rebels. Non-stop attacks were made during May and into June, 43 Squadron alone flying more than 150 sorties, and firing 1,000 rockets and 50,000 rounds of ammunition. The air war had certainly become more 'exciting', as Sqn Ldr Phil Champniss, CO 43 Squadron, confirms:

> The attack on Fort Harib started sparking all sorts of hoo-hah and then we went into the Radfan business. A very exciting time, and for 43 Squadron, certainly, extremely tiring. There were several days where I flew four and five sorties a day, so we must have been flying thirty to thirty-five sorties a day, perhaps more. We had this phrase: 'Air Proscription'. There were really two sorts of sortie during the Radfan. There were the pre-planned strike targets, i.e. political ones – a house, a fort, a collection of houses, all of which were deemed to be worthy of knocking down. We had photographs of them but they weren't very much use because they were always taken at very low level. When you are up high that's not much good to you but we did have Forward Air Controllers. Those targets were pre-planned and were politically chosen, such as a local headman who needed to be taught a lesson. That's how it was and so we'd go up and give him a bit of a belt.

Hunter close air support was very much in demand, and the accuracy of the RAF pilots was lauded by ground troops in the Protectorate. Following a fact-finding visit to Aden, Hugh Fraser, Minister of State for the RAF, said: 'The skill and accuracy of the aircrew is such that the troops in forward areas are calling down RAF fighters to strike dissident strongholds only 25 yards from their own positions. Considering the nature of the terrain, a 25-yard margin is incredible.'

By mid-1964 the dissident tribes had one by one sued for peace. On 18 November 1964, following a series of rocket and cannon strafing attacks by the Hunters, the last remaining dissident tribe capitulated. Fighting continued in Aden itself and the Hunters were kept busy until finally, in 1967, Britain withdrew from Aden. No. 43 Squadron flew its last ground-attack sorties on 9 November 1967 before being disbanded as a Hunter squadron. Subsequently 8 and 208 Squadrons formed the Offensive Support Wing at Muharraq in Bahrain, with 8 Squadron receiving 1417 Flight's Hunter FR.10s on 29 November. The Hunters remained at Muharraq until 1971 when British forces made their final withdrawal from the Arabian Gulf. No. 208 Squadron disbanded on 10 September 1971 and its Hunters were transferred to 8 Squadron at Sharjah, providing support for the remaining British troops and the Trucial Oman Scouts until the end of the year, when the squadron disbanded. No. 8 Squadron re-formed as a Shackleton AEW2 unit on New Year's Day 1972.

Another 'hot-spot' in the 1960s was in the Far East, where Indonesia had a policy of 'confrontation' (rather than all-out war) against the new Malaysian Federation, created in December 1962. In particular the policy was aimed at the incorporation of West Malaysia into the Federation, as the whole of Borneo was regarded as Indonesian, and there were armed uprisings in Brunei and Sarawak. British forces were based in Singapore and Malaysia as part of the South East Asia Treaty Organisation (SEATO). No. 20 Squadron, which disbanded on 30 December 1960 and re-formed at Tengah, Singapore, on 1 September 1961 with sixteen FGA.9s plus two T.7s, provided day

FGA.9 XF376 of 208 Squadron flying low over the Aden Protectorate. In October 1976 XF376 joined the TWU at Brawdy. (via *Ben Jones*)

D. H-H.

'We (Air Movements) did not have a lot to do with 8 and 208 Squadrons in Muharraq. The Hunters weren't noted for their cargo/passenger carrying ability (!) but their pilots used to arrive and depart like the rest of us courtesy of Air Support Command, latterly usually a VC10 known locally as the "moon rocket" and still going strong. There was one which came in from UK on a Wednesday evening on a QTR (quick turn round – pan 1). One Dai Heather-Hayes was scheduled to depart tour-ex on this particular evening but come chocks time, despite searches of the mess bar and other likely places he could not be found. All other passengers were aboard and eventually the captain decided he had to go. The steps were taken away and he moved off. At this point a Land Rover came on to the airfield at some speed. Out leapt D. H-H. (who was not unlike the actor Richard Harris in appearance and demeanour), umbrella in one hand, Arabian musket in the other, frantically waving both. The captain obviously saw this "whirling Dervish" and stopped as his progress was being impeded. We confirmed to Ops that this was the missing passenger. Ops relayed the info to the captain who most obligingly I thought, relayed back a request for steps, which were duly pushed out, and H-H. boarded, with or without "normal" luggage I do not recall!

'This type of "entertaining" behaviour was not wholly typical of the Hunter boys who by and large were a pretty responsible lot, whilst at work anyway. Most other memories relate to mess nights, e.g. jousting with mops on Honda 50s up and down the ante room and the memorable effect that a Hunter starter cartridge has when fired (concealed and packed beneath many pounds of flour) adjacent to the top dining table. Not surprisingly, the firing wires were traced to the seat occupied by the aforementioned H-H. if I remember correctly! Perhaps more surprisingly, I have no recollection of disciplinary action but then our CO was Group Captain "Twinkle" Storey!'

Chris Lampard, Air Movements, RAF Muharraq, 1967–8

Two FGA.9s, 'E' and 'G' of 8 Squadron, over RAF Muharraq, Bahrain, in 1968. (*Chris Lampard*)

fighter/ground-attack for the whole theatre. No. 28 Squadron, which in June–August 1962 received FGA.9s in place of its DH Venom FB.4s, was based at Kai Tak in Hong Kong with four FGA.9s plus one T.7. The SEATO air component was responsible for countering Indonesian Air Force (IAF) incursions over Malaysia. Although the IAF comprised mostly obsolete F-51 Mustangs and B-25 Mitchell bombers, it was equipped with a number of Soviet fighter and bomber aircraft. (A Hunter and a MiG-17 actually chased each other around the sky on one occasion although no shots were fired.) A greater

RAF and RAAF presence ensued when Indonesian-backed guerrillas began infiltrating Malaysian territory in September 1963. Then the stakes were raised with RAF Victor bombers being sent to the region.

Sqn Ldr (now Air Cdre) G. 'Max' McA. Bacon was OC 20 Squadron from 3 April 1964 to 16 December 1965. He recalls:

As confrontation escalated, political restrictions in the UK meant that forward-firing weapons only were likely to be permitted to be used against Indonesian targets. This meant that the main attack aircraft, the Canberras, were unable to use their 1,000lb bombs, thus limiting them to 2-inch rocket pods. The Hunter's four 30mm Aden cannon and twelve or sixteen 3-inch RP [rockets] then became the heaviest weapons that could be used. Whilst the Canberra had a much better radius of action than the Hunter, it was vulnerable to Indonesian air defence (Mustangs and MiG 21s in the main) and so within the Hunter's radius of action joint formations were planned accordingly. Early in 1964 the Indonesian

Air Force flew Tu.16 Badgers over East Malaysia and Indonesian ground forces made penetrations of West Malaysian territory. Accordingly British Army units were deployed on the border and Javelin and Hunter border patrols were flown based on either Kuching [the capital and port of Sarawak state on the Sarawak River] and/or Labuan [a flat, wooded island off north-west Borneo]. The Javelins operated by night and the Hunters by day.

Left and overleaf: Two views of FGA.9s XJ695/K and XJ690/G of 20 Squadron on anti-infiltration patrol near Pulau Tioman off the east coast of Malaysia in September 1965. XJ690 was delivered to 20 Squadron, after conversion from F.6 to FGA.9, on 27 October 1964. It was re-purchased by Hawker Siddeley Aircraft in February 1976. XJ695 was delivered to 20 Squadron, after conversion from F.6 to FGA.9, on 15 January 1965. It joined the TWU at Brawdy in October 1976 after serving with 45 and 58 Squadrons at Wittering. (via *GMS*)

Indonesian propaganda flights over North Borneo had increased and on 20 February 1964 four Hunter FGA.9s of 20 Squadron had each detached to Labuan and Kuching to fly surveillance and CAP in the Air Defence Identification Zone (ADIZ) encompassing Sabah (formerly North Borneo) and Sarawak. On three days, 23, 24 and 26 December 1964, FGA.9s of 20 Squadron and Canberras of 45 Squadron mounted real and simulated air strikes on the terrorists to sap their morale and disperse them into smaller groups to be more easily dealt with by the security forces. In August 1964 tension increased dramatically when Indonesian paratroops landed in force in Western Malaysia.

On 2 September, 96 Indonesian paratroops were dropped by three C-130s near Labis in north-central Johore. The enemy was located and the next day the FGA.9s, each armed with sixteen 3-inch RPs fitted with semi-armour-piercing warheads, went into action. They flew fourteen sorties and the rocket and cannon firing strikes went on for several more days. Results were unknown as 1km squares of jungle were attacked with no particular targets in sight but by the end of September almost all the Indonesian troops had been either killed or captured.

Thereafter Indonesian incursions in Malaysia were smaller and more sporadic: forty-one landings and sabotage attempts were made

FGA.9s XJ683/F and XJ690/G of 20 Squadron from RAF Tengah, Singapore, in 1965. XJ683 was built at Kingston as an F.6 and first flew on 7 February 1957 in the hands of Don Lucey before being delivered to the RAF on 29 March 1957. It first served with 93 Squadron and later, after conversion to FGA.9, with 43 Squadron. XJ690, which was also converted from F.6 to FGA.9, flew for the first time on 12 February 1957 and operated with 14 Squadron before delivery as an FGA.9 to 20 Squadron on 27 October 1964. Hawker Siddeley Aircraft purchased it in February 1976. (Richard Wilson)

FGA.9s led by XJ690/G taxiing out at RAF Tengah, Singapore, for the flight to RAAF Butterworth, Penang, for 20 Squadron's annual APC (Armament Practice Camp), 25 June 1966. (*Neal J. Wharton*)

between August 1964 and March 1965 by just over 700 infiltrators. During 1964–5 Javelins of 60 and 64 Squadrons flew night and all-weather patrols over the Indonesian coast while the FGA.9s of 20 Squadron, operating from Tengah, carried out rocket strikes and strafing attacks on guerrilla concentrations in the southern end of the Malay peninsula. When some Indonesian troops landed at Bukit Pengerang east of Changi on the night of 30 April/1 May 1965, and quickly gained a foothold in an old Second World War Japanese fortification to await further reinforcements, four FGA.9s directed by a Forward Air Controller made rocket and cannon strafing attacks to dislodge them. Thirteen infiltrators were captured and the rest captured or killed later. On 1 September 1965 two B-25 Mitchells at Pa Umor, 100 miles south of Labuan, were strafed. A month later a Whirlwind helicopter was shot down 30 miles south of Kuching and four extra Hunters were sent to the

Sarawak base. From October 1965 RAAF Sabres started to take over border patrol and escort duties from the Hunters and were introduced to the topography and the weather by 20 Squadron.

Sqn Ldr Max Bacon concludes:

During my time we had three aircraft written off and one pilot was killed. Flt Lt Peter Martin ejected overhead Tengah airfield [on 21 April 1964] while practising a solo aerobatic display he was to give at Bangkok. The event was spectacular and the aircraft ejector seat and pilot all landed safely on the airfield causing no damage or injury. The engine had failed while the aircraft was flying inverted due to a recuperator bag failure. Flg Off Douglas Clavering was lost one misty morning [19 September 1964] while flying low level patrols just to the south of Singapore guarding against Indonesian surprise attacks. No cause was determined but on the day it was difficult to see a horizon, particularly when looking out for hostile forces and doing steep turns to stay in the required position. Flt Lt Heinz Frick ejected after getting into a spin while practising air combat [19 October 1964]. He sensibly ejected when he was getting too low to guarantee recovery.

'Royal Air Force searchers have found the wreckage of a Hawker Hunter fighter, which crashed in a swamp near Batu Pahat in Johore on Monday while on a training flight. An RAF spokesman said that a Board of Inquiry would decide whether to salvage the one-seater plane from which its pilot, Flying Officer H. Frick, escaped by ejaculating [*sic*] himself and then wading from the swamp to the beach where he was later picked up by a helicopter. FO Frick was treated at Changi Hospital for a strained back.'

Straits Times, *October 1964*

At squadron level we made several modifications to the Hunter FGA.9. To make the bounce aircraft more visible to those being bounced, during practice air combat we had two nose-cones covered in dayglo orange fablon. Unfortunately at air combat speeds this was stripped off and so we used bright yellow paint instead. The nose-cones could be swapped quite quickly so if an aircraft went unserviceable on start up, the yellow nose could be put on the spare aircraft with little delay.

With all our deployments to Borneo, there was always a need to ferry parts or items of personal equipment so we painted an outboard 100-gallon drop-tank red and fitted it when necessary. Unfortunately Flt Lt Dick Smith had an undercarriage leg stay retracted when he was landing at Kuching and although he made an excellent two-wheel landing, the engineering staff at HQ were very upset to see we had an unofficial drop-tank fitted. In fact it probably protected the aircraft from being damaged.

Although 81 Squadron's Canberras provided photographic reconnaissance there was no fighter reconnaissance in theatre, so I arranged for a spare nose-cone to be fitted with a sideways-looking F95 camera with a glass window. It was necessary to remove the normal radar-ranging equipment but then the nose-cone was quick to fit and gave us a new capability. By the time I left the squadron we had not investigated demisting the glass panel but I understand the modification was changed in due course.

Compared to Aden, distances in the Far East were much greater. I flew Venoms in Aden, and the Yemen border (Radfan) was only about 170nm [nautical miles] away and the Wadi Hadrumat 270nm. By comparison, from Tengah we were regularly deploying to Kuching (430nm) and Labuan (730nm). Despite the long distances we flew

(we often did high-low-high dummy attacks on bridges near the Thai border 310nm from Tengah), the winds were normally very light and there was no magnetic variation to affect our compass heading. We had no real navigation aids until we were within radio range of an airfield. Nevertheless if one flew an accurate heading at an accurate speed for a pre-planned time the destination would come up as calculated. At low level we cruised at 420 knots (= 7 miles per minute) so we marked our maps in minutes to know just where we were.

Our task in Borneo was to deter and if necessary shoot down any Indonesian Air Force overflights of East Malaysia, and to escort transport aircraft on supply drops. Although a Javelin did meet a C-130 flying down a valley, we never did. Nor did we see the Mitchells, which made a sneak attack on Borneo. There was such a huge border area to cover (the Malaysian/Indonesian border is about 1,100nm long) so there wasn't much chance of guaranteeing to prevent Indonesian penetrations along its length. Normally we flew border patrols at 250 knots (the best range speed) but were on the lookout for Mustangs. Our tactic then was to drop our tanks and manoeuvre in the vertical plane as they would easily be able to turn inside us but lacked our climbing ability. Border patrols in the early morning were very difficult as valleys were normally full of

Biggles vs. the MiG

'If there is despondency in the gallant rank and file of the Royal Air Force today, it can be explained by an intelligent reading of its production programme and its present strike-fighter performance. Without peering into the future and asking what aircraft the RAF will have in the seventies, it is no exaggeration to say that its operational Hunter aircraft Mk 9 compares with other NATO strike fighter forces much as a London taxicab compares with the best racing model. In South-East Asia, where Britain sometimes appears to be on the brink of war with President Sukarno, the Hunter would have to fight the MiG-21, which flies 700mph faster than the maximum speed of the Hunter. What sort of confrontation would that be? The supersonic Lightning is simply a home defence type and has no strike capability.'

Daily Telegraph, *30 December 1964*

An FGA.9 of 20 Squadron with T.7 XF310 behind, at RAAF Butterworth, July 1966. XF310 was built as an F.4 and was used in experimental trials of the Fairey Fireflash missile installation prior to being converted to a two-seater. (*Neal J. Wharton*)

FGA.9s of 20 Squadron lined up at RAAF Butterworth in July 1966. (*Neal J. Wharton*)

low cloud but the Hunter could normally escape from being trapped by using full power and climbing steeply. Less highly powered aircraft risked hitting mountains if they flew into valleys covered in cloud.

The weather was quite different between Kuching and Labuan. Each day large cumulo-nimbus clouds would develop but because Kuching was inland from the coast, they would form over the airfield. As there was no real diversion airfield it was not unusual to come back from an afternoon border patrol to find the airfield closed due to heavy rain. All one could then do was to hold off, hoping the rain would stop. If not, one had to divert to Singapore some 300 miles away. This normally meant dropping the 230-gallon tanks to improve our cruising fuel consumption. There were quite a number of these tanks in the South China Sea.

At Labuan the thunder-clouds built up inland and often drifted over the airfield during the night. Only the maritime Shackleton patrols were hindered and they had so much fuel they could wait for an hour or so for a clearance. A sensitive area of East Borneo was the town of Tawau at the north-east corner. On several occasions the Indonesians would position a ship with troops behind an island on their side of the border. Accordingly, we flew reinforcements from Tengah to Labuan so we could overfly to deter any attack. On one occasion our reinforcements couldn't get to Labuan before dark so we landed six aircraft on the 6,000ft runway using our braking parachutes. I was somewhat concerned as several pilots were not in night-flying practice, but all went well.

The unofficial war largely fizzled out and the confrontation finally ended on 11 August 1966 with the signing of a peace treaty. Late in December 28 Squadron disbanded at Kai Tak, later re-forming as a helicopter squadron in April 1968. During January–December 1969 three Pioneer CCI aircraft were employed by 20 Squadron in a very successful FAC role. No. 20 Squadron remained at RAF Tengah until February 1970.

In Britain meanwhile, 1 and 54 Squadrons at Stradishall had finally begun exchanging their F.6s for FGA.9s in early 1961. The Stradishall

Pilots of 20 Squadron strapping-in on the line at Tengah prior to the Battle of Britain flypast over Singapore on 17 September 1966. In the foreground is Spitfire DW-X of the Hong Kong Historic Flight with Flt Lt Phil Dacre of 20 Squadron in the cockpit. After the disbandment of 28 Squadron (Hunters), based in Hong Kong, 20 Squadron maintained a small detachment of Hunters in the colony. Flights to Hong Kong routed via Labuan, Sabah and Clarke AFB, Philippines. (*Neal J. Wharton*)

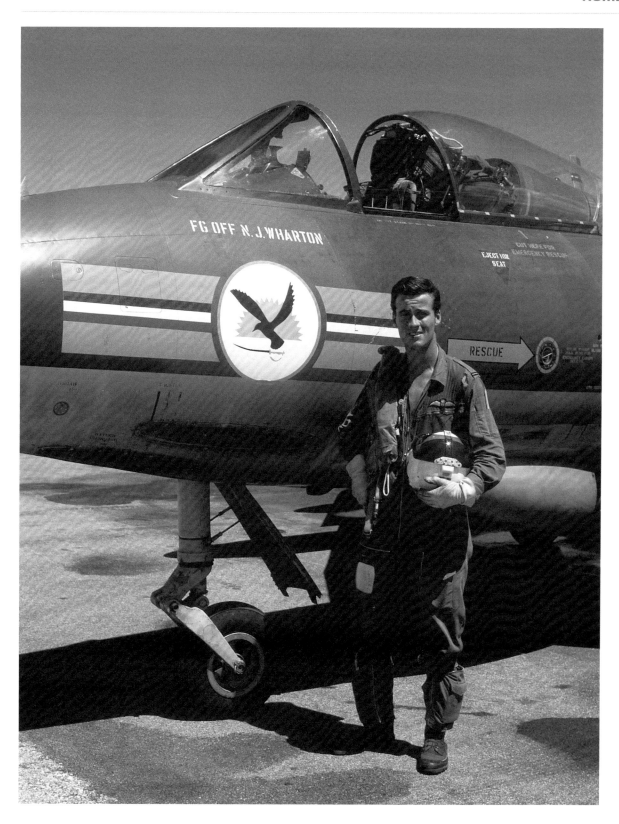

Overleaf: A pair of 20 Squadron Hunters in transit from Labuan to Clarke AFB in the Philippines on 22 May 1968. (*Neal J. Wharton*)

Homeward bound. Flg Off Neal Wharton of 20 Squadron beside his Hunter at Labuan (next stop Tengah) on 5 June 1968. Periodically squadron pilots' names were stencilled on to the side of the aircraft during maintenance schedules. By pure coincidence Neal Wharton was flying his 'own' aircraft on this occasion. He joined 20 Squadron as a first tourist in June 1966 (aged 20), later flying Hunters and Harriers on 1 Squadron, 233 OCU and 3 Squadron, followed by Gnats and Hawks with the Red Arrows from 1979 to 1981. (*Neal J. Wharton*)

Spot the Hunter! Finals for Runway 13 at Kai Tak Airport, Hong Kong, 3 June 1968. (*Neal J. Wharton*)

Withdrawal from Empire

'The sands of time are running out, the best station (from the operational point of view) changes as the financiers withdraw their credit in order to maintain funds in the UK. So 20 Squadron together with 45 Squadron say goodbye to RAF Tengah. No. 81 Squadron has already disbanded. We wish you well Tengah on the 19th February; along with 45, 74 and 81 Squadrons we felt that we were Tengah . . .'

Sqn Ldr C.J. Strong, CO 20 Squadron, writing in the Tengah Times*, February 1970*

On 18 February, 20 Squadron disbanded. It had served for over fifty-one years, thirty-five of them in Asia. No. 45 Squadron, which operated Canberra bombers, disbanded the same day but in 1972 was re-formed as a Hunter squadron.

Wing was to form the offensive air component of 38 Group Tactical Support Wing, RAF Transport Command. In November 1961, still not fully re-equipped, the F.6, FGA.9 and T.7 aircraft of 1 and 54 Squadrons left Stradishall for their new station at RAF Waterbeach, Cambridgeshire. In December the two squadrons became part of HQ 38 Group, the RAF's contribution to the Allied Command Europe Mobile Forces, dedicated to the rapid reinforcement of the NATO flanks. Their role was honed to perfection with air firing at ranges in The Wash and with low-level flying and navigational training during a number of exercises in the UK and overseas. Early in 1963 54 Squadron's FGA.9s carried out border patrol duties along the Yemen border until relieved by 43 Squadron's FGA.9s. In August 1 and

54 Squadrons moved from Waterbeach and relocated to West Raynham, Norfolk, from where they deployed overseas on several occasions. In the early 1960s the Hunters took part in air defence and reinforcement exercises in the Mediterranean and West Germany, and on occasion, when General Franco applied political pressure against Gibraltar, they increased the RAF presence at the Rock with three- and four-week detachments.

In March 1967 the Raynham Hunters were among the aircraft called upon to try to disperse oil on troubled waters. On 18 March the 61,000-ton supertanker *Torrey Canyon* had crashed into the Seven Stones Reef off Land's End, and began leaking her entire cargo of 118,000 tons of crude oil from the Middle East. All attempts to refloat the tanker failed and over the next nine days the heavy Atlantic rollers broke the tanker into three pieces, each piece spewing slicks of the cargo into the English Channel. The Royal Navy and RAF were ordered to burn as much oil as possible before it could leak out of the wrecked tanker. On 28 March HS Buccaneer S.2s of 800 and 736 Squadrons from RNAS Brawdy bombed the wreck with great accuracy and set it on fire. Relays of Hunters from 229 OCU at Chivenor dropped 100-gallon tanks containing kerosene to stoke up the blaze, but the oil refused to burn.

Next morning three FGA.9s of 1 Squadron, flown by Sqn Ldr G. 'Spike' Jones, the CO, and Flt Lt B.K. 'Wally' Walton and Flt Lt Alan Pollock, each carrying two 100-gallon drop-tanks filled with napalm on the outboard wing pylons, set out to bomb the *Torrey Canyon*. The tanks were released explosively from the pylons by 'pickling' (pressing the bombing button), which fired the

Wg Cdr Mike Hobson, OC Flying Wing and Chief Instructor 229 OCU Chivenor, pictured on 20 November 1964 next to a 28 Squadron Hunter at Kai Tak, Hong Kong. Mike recalls: 'As the Hunter OCU, one of our tasks was the standardization of all Hunter squadrons, so we would fly out to Germany, the Middle East and the Far East on an annual basis to fly with a selection of their pilots. The first time that I ever landed at Kai Tak was from a sector recce in a Hunter 7, and it was an eye-opening experience to find oneself on the final approach flying between the rooftops with lines of washing flapping on each side during the descent!
OC 28 Squadron was Sqn Ldr 'Bodger' Edwards, and on his last sortie at Chivenor before going out to take over the squadron, contrary to standard procedure I had approved his leading a four-ship formation on a low flying ground-attack exercise. This seemed reasonable, as he was about to become a squadron commander. Unfortunately on the final leg his aircraft had an argument with some high-tension cables, causing a large part of Devon to be blacked out for a while. I recall having a bit of explaining to do to Command Headquarters who considered that he should not now get command of 28 Squadron. However, we won in the end, and he went out as planned, looking after me royally when I later arrived in Hong Kong on the standardization visit.' (*Mike Hobson*)

'[Wg Cdr Mike Hobson was posted as OC Flying Wing and Chief Instructor to 229 OCU Chivenor on 13 January 1963.] But first I had to spend two months on a flying refresher course at RAF Manby and Strubby, as it was just over four years since I had been on a flying appointment. I completed a shortened version of the Hunter Conversion Course, stepping into the "chair" in late May of that year. There were a few rumblings around the Command about my appointment, as it was the first time ever that it had been filled by a non-QFI. I thought that it showed a remarkable flair of practicality! During my time at Chivenor we trained many Rhodesians (it was just before UDI) and practically the whole of the Kuwaiti and Indian Defence Force. It was hard on some of these students during the winter months. Chivenor was a hutted camp and they had to go outside for the toilets and ablutions, so that many of them were off flying with heavy colds for considerable periods, and we had to work hard to get the courses through on time. We also ran an ongoing series of FAC (Forward Air Controller) courses for the Army, when we would fly them in Hunter 7s on ground-attack exercises to show them what it was like from the pilot's point of view. We learned very quickly always to have a handy supply of sick-bags! The only serious accident while I was at Chivenor resulted in a fatality when Flt Lt Rao of the Indian Air Force crashed into the sea off Hartland Point after losing contact with his leader during a pairs GCA. That was on 17 February 1964.'

'[Wg Cdr Mike Hobson left Chivenor on 3 June 1965.] On the day after I handed over the Flying Wing my wife Barbara and son Rick were catching the train from the station at nearby Wrafton, so I ran them there in the car to see them off. As we set off, at approximately 0900 hr, I could hear no sound of flying, which was unusual, as our first sorties were normally off by 0800 hr at the latest. "Oh well," I thought, "it just goes to show – as soon as I leave, the whole place goes to pot!" However, we got to the station, and just as the train appeared and was drawing into the platform, a distant rumble grew into a great roar, and thirty-two Hunters and four Meteors flew directly over us. I am not ashamed to say that I had a lump in my throat and a tear in my eye – it was a moment never to be forgotten. It is also, to the best of my knowledge, the largest number of Hunters ever to have been seen in close formation, either before or since. Apparently some of the chaps had been working voluntarily through the night to achieve the serviceability required.'

Wg Cdr Mike Hobson

Wg Cdr Hobson completed the Joint Services Staff College course at Latimer and then returned to the OCU to do an eight-sortie refresher course – with seven of the sorties flown in two days! – before going to RAF Coltishall to take over 226 Lightning OCU. At the time of writing his son Rick is W/C Hobson, OC 24 Squadron, flying the C-130J Hercules.

Hunters of 229 OCU on the line at Chivenor in November 1964. Note the reserve squadron crest on the nose and the white painted spine of the nearest Hunter. (*Mike Hobson*)

Explosive Release Unit (ERU). 'Spike' Jones's drop-tanks failed to ignite the surface oil, but Walton's started a huge fireball, which forced Alan Pollock to abort his run. He came around again and dropped his napalm as soon as he entered the smoke. The unexpectedly massive, explosive thump to his wings as the napalm tanks were exploded off convinced him that he had hit the ship's mast. Pollock burst out of the black inferno, safe, into the sunlight beyond the Seven Stones Reef. The small fires soon went out. More napalm strikes were mounted in the afternoon, preceded by two Hunters firing salvoes of twelve 3-inch rockets to burst the ship's tanks. Six aircraft made a further twelve napalm bombing attacks on the afternoon of the 30th but they were unsuccessful and air operations were suspended that evening.

The formation of RAF Strike Command from Fighter and Bomber Commands on 30 April 1968 left two 'NATO mobile' FGA.9 squadrons, nos 1 and 54, within 38 Group and Air Support Command, as their tactical support and strike force punch. The year 1968 was also memorable in that the RAF celebrated its fiftieth anniversary on Monday 1 April. Though formal parades would mark the event, a fly-past planned in conjunction with the Lancaster House dinner with the queen was cancelled at the last moment as 'inappropriate'. But 32-year-old pilot Flt Lt Alan Pollock of 1 Squadron at West Raynham was not alone in thinking that a flypast over London was more appropriate to the occasion:

Since nothing else was going to happen from an airborne point of view I prevailed on the Boss, Sqn Ldr Spike Jones, that we should carry out celebration anniversary leaflet raids . . . Immediately after the parade on 1 April we 'bombed up' the aircraft with a celebration warload of anniversary leaflets in the flaps, and an adequate supply of 4½-inch GP ('Government property') bog-rolls stowed in the airbrake. My Hunter was first up using a flapless take-off technique and, despite a strong gusty crosswind, by getting down below the side of the hangar I was fortunate to have a good drop above 54 Squadron's pilots outside their crew room at West Raynham. The station was then given a beat-up from the south, with pull-up into a vertical roll.

One of our best pilots and weaponeers, Flt Lt 'Wally' Walton, was selected for Wattisham, another proud fighter base and home for part of the Lightning force. An ex-Lightning OCU pilot from Coltishall, Ken Becker, was suitably chosen for the paper delivery there. Successful drops were also made by our ex-Vietnam F-105 pilot and USAF exchange officer, Capt Pete Albrecht at Chivenor and by Flg Off Barry Horton in bad weather at Valley.

FGA.9 XF442 at the 19 Squadron Lightning F.2 base at RAF Leconfield, Yorkshire, in September 1965. Behind is Douglas C-54A-15-DC G-ASOG of Air Ferry Ltd, which was being used to help move the Lightning squadron to its new home at RAF Gütersloh in Germany. (G-ASOG crashed 5km short of Frankfurt Airport on 21 January 1967.) XF442 was built at Baginton as an F.6 and it served originally with 247 and 43 Squadrons before being returned to Hawker Siddeley on 1 June 1959 for conversion to FGA.9. It was flown for the first time in its new mark by Flt Lt Tilak on 10 March 1960 and in 1962 was used for air firing trials with rocket projectiles. XF442 also served with 1 Squadron. On 5 April 1968, while returning to West Raynham from a visit to Tangmere, XF442, piloted by Flt Lt Alan Pollock, rocked its wings in salute to the RAF Memorial on the London Embankment before flying under the upper span of Tower Bridge! In 1971 XF442 joined 8 Squadron, moving to 2 TWU in 1980. (*John Hale*)

Chivenor and Valley telephoned their congratulations but Wattisham (with an AOC's inspection next day) and Coltishall complained of 'dangerous flying, bad example, untidy debris and poor airmanship from No. 1!' A pair of Lightnings from Wattisham dropped toilet rolls on West Raynham in a 'retaliatory raid'. It was all good inter-squadron rivalry, but by the end of the week squadron 'high jinks' really overstepped the mark.

On 5 April, while returning to West Raynham from a visit to RAF Tangmere, F.6 XF442, piloted by Flt Lt Pollock, No. 4 in the lead section of four Hunters, broke away from the formation immediately after take-off, and headed for the City of London. He circled Whitehall and then proceeded to put the power on as he passed the Houses of Parliament where a debate was in progress. Three times he circled, then, on the final orbit, he levelled out again over the Thames and dipped his wings in salute to the RAF Memorial on the London Embankment, before making his intended exit to the east. Pollock recalls:

> Until this very instant, I'd had absolutely no idea that of course Tower Bridge would be in my low-level path but the idea of flying through the spans suddenly struck me. It was easy enough but how to do it with safety for those on the bridge? With eight seconds to grapple with, then execute, the seductive proposition, time seemed to stand still. Few ground-attack pilots of any nationality could have resisted. My brain raced, swooping low over the Pool of London to solve this instant safety puzzle, as a red double-decker bus began crossing the bridge from stage left. The Hunter and years of fast low-level strike flying made the decision simple. Approaching the famous structure downstream at over 300mph, I began an inverse bombing run, with my target cues above rather than below. I aimed for my fin tip just to miss Tower Bridge's upper steel span, as I flew, four seconds later as high above the traffic as possible, through the top centre of the 110ft deep, 200ft wide gap framed by its towers and bascules!'

Pollock then flew homeward, making celebratory flag-wave beat-ups at Wattisham, Lakenheath

F.6 XJ713 of 229 OCU at Hatfield on 13 July 1968. This Hunter was flown for the first time on 22 February 1957 by Duncan Simpson and it went on to serve with 20, 14 and 1 Squadrons before being purchased by Hawkers on 10 September 1969 for conversion to FGA.71 (as 722). It was delivered to the Chilean Air Force on 21 December 1970. (*Adrian Balch*)

F.6 XF509 of 4 FTS at RAF Gütersloh in September 1973. Behind is XF383. XF509 was a Baginton-built F.6, first issued to 54 Squadron before moving to Bristol for use as a chase plane for the Fairey FD-2 conversion. In about 1965 XF509 moved to 4 FTS. XF383 served with 1, 65 and 263 Squadrons and 229 OCU before joining 4 FTS in 1968. (*Adrian Balch*)

and Marham. Finally, and with less than 400lb of fuel remaining, he carried out a 'rather hurried, inadequate, inverted run over the squadron hangars at RAF West Raynham before breaking downwind, punching down the gear and landing'. The errant pilot taxied in, expecting a formal reception committee. None appeared and he went to phone his wife and family. 'The balloon's possibly gone up,' he said dryly to the station switchboard girl. Then he went to see the CO, OC Flying and the station commander, to tell them what they already knew. 'Spike Jones seemed strangely relieved that Whitehall wasn't littered with leaflets,' recalls Pollock. But it was no laughing matter. West Raynham hit the world's headlines and for Flt Lt Pollock, who subsequently received a medical discharge, it was the end of his flying career in the RAF.

On 18 July 1969, 1 Squadron left West Raynham for Wittering to begin conversion to the Harrier, but 54 Squadron, which was expected to become the second Harrier squadron at Wittering, was instead disbanded on 1 September 1969. Its Hunter pilots became the UK echelon of 4 Squadron while a new 54 Squadron was formed, equipped with the Phantom FGR.2. In 1974 54 Squadron re-formed again, this time with the Jaguar GR.1.

The last FGA.9s meanwhile were finally withdrawn from first-line service when 8 Squadron returned to the UK from the Gulf to disband at the end of 1971. However, Britain's withdrawal from 'east of Suez' and the passing of the Hunter and Canberra squadrons brought unforeseen problems. Whereas recently qualified pilots once cut their operational teeth on jets like the Hunter, now they were going straight from fast-jet OCUs to squadrons equipped with more sophisticated types, notably the Phantom, Harrier and Buccaneer, and, in the near future, the Jaguar tactical strike and reconnaissance aircraft. Another problem was that a surplus of jet pilots

---

The Blue Herons

From 1962 Hunters began to be replaced in first-line RAF service both at home and abroad by the Lightning F.2 and the Canberra B(1)8. Forty Hunters, all F.4s, were converted to GA.11s for the Fleet Air Arm and issued to 738 Training Squadron at RNAS Lossiemouth and Brawdy for ground-attack training duties. Lossiemouth began taking delivery of the GA.11 in June 1962. Nos 759 and 764 Squadrons were also similarly equipped. In 1967 three Hunter GA.11s and a Hunter T.8 from 738 Squadron formed a FAA aerobatic team. Eight years later, in July 1975, the Blue Herons aerobatic team was formed when four GA.11s were flown by civilian pilots of Airwork Services, based at RNAS Yeovilton (otherwise known as HMS *Heron*).

This was believed to be the first aerobatic team in the world in which civilian pilots flew military jet fighter aircraft. The Hunter GA.11 aircraft (7575lb thrust) flown by the team were operated by Airwork Services Limited, under contract to the Royal Navy, who provided aircrew and engineering personnel to fly and service them.

The unit was known as the FRADU (Fleet Requirements and Air Direction Unit), flying Hunter GA.11s and T.8s and also Canberra TT1Bs and T.22s. It is the function of FRADU to assist ships of the Royal Navy and many foreign navies to work up to full operational status by carrying out Radio/Radar trials, visual and Radar Tracking followed by live shoots.

Practice interceptions at high and low levels are provided to train RN Officers as fighter controllers, aircraft are also provided for use by RN Officers of the Naval Flying Standards flight also based at RNAS Yeovilton. All the pilots were ex-RAF or ex-RN, a mixture of light and dark blue.

Overleaf: WW654, XE682, WT806 and WT804 of the Blue Herons over RNAS Yeovilton in 1976. (*Richard Wilson*)

T.12 XE531 of the RAE at Greenham Common on 2 August 1976. This Kingston-built F.6 was flown for the first time on 9 January 1956 by Hugh Merewether and was used by the Ministry of Supply in tropical trials before returning to Hawkers in 1959 for conversion to FGA.9 standard. When in 1962 Hawker Siddeley received an order from the MoS for a two-seat Hunter with a 200-series Avon to carry out avionics trials for the BAC TSR.2, XE531 was refurbished to two-seat configuration and fitted with a Specto Avionics head-up display (HUD) and a vertical nose camera. In 1963 XE531 became the only Hunter Mk 12 in existence, though others were expected to follow to train operational TSR.2 aircrew. Before this could happen, however, the TSR.2 project was cancelled in 1965. XE531 was retained by the RAE as a trials aircraft at Farnborough and Thurleigh (Bedford) for development work on the Harrier, during which time it operated with an early 'fly by wire' system. XE531 crashed on take-off at Farnborough on 17 March 1983. (*Adrian Balch*)

GA.11 XF301 of 764 Squadron (RN) at Culdrose on 28 July 1971. This Blackpool-built F.4 was delivered on 30 December 1955 and issued to 43 Squadron. It was converted to GA.11 and delivered in October 1962, transferring to 738 Squadron in November 1964. (*Adrian Balch*)

GA.11 XF977 of 764 Squadron (RN) at Lossiemouth on 17 April 1970. Built at Blackpool as an F.4, XF977 was delivered to the RAF on 17 May 1956, and joined 118 Squadron of the 2nd TAF at Jever, where it became the personal aircraft of the CO, Sqn Ldr Norman C.P. Buddin. After the squadron disbanded, XF977/A joined the Sylt Station Flight and then, in 1962, the aircraft returned to Hawkers for conversion to GA.11 standard. It was delivered to RNAS Lossiemouth on 2 October 1962, joining 764 Squadron in 1969. From 1974 it operated with FRADU at Yeovilton. (*Adrian Balch*)

GA.11 XE707 of FRADU at Hurn on 6 August 1971. XE707 was originally an F.4 built at Blackpool and delivered to the RAF on 1 September 1955. It served with 93 and 118 Squadrons and was converted to GA.11 before being issued to 738 Squadron in August 1964. It joined 764 Squadron in November 1964 and went on to serve with FRU and FRADU. (*Adrian Balch*)

T.7 XL618 of 229 OCU at RAF Chivenor on 7 August 1971. This aircraft was flown for the first time on 10 January 1959 by David Lockspeiser and was delivered to the RAF on 4 February 1959. It operated with the Gütersloh and Jever Station Flights before joining 229 OCU in April 1964. It transferred to RAF Brawdy in November 1976. (*Adrian Balch*)

F.6 XF386 of 234 Squadron and 229 OCU at Chivenor on 7 August 1971. Before joining the OCU in April 1961 this aircraft also served with 65 and 92 Squadrons. (*Adrian Balch*)

leaving Flying Training School (FTS) was creating a long, inactive flying period before they could enter OCU. This delay could seriously impair their progress and adversely affect their newly acquired skills. Both problems could be solved with the introduction of a short post-graduate tour, which would prepare these young pilots, especially those who would fly the Jaguar, with some experience in the low-level tactical environment before they joined the fast-jet OCUs. As an interim measure it was announced on 22 June 1972 that two fully operational DF/GA (day fighter/ground-attack) squadrons equipped with Hunters would fulfil this tactical training role, and they would be based at Wittering (once the runway there had been resurfaced).

On 1 August 1972, 45 Squadron, the senior inactive Hunter squadron, re-formed at West Raynham with eight FGA.9s and a T.7, moving to Wittering on 29 September that year. From June 1973 the training syllabus included Dissimilar Air Combat Training (DACT) with Phantoms, Lightnings and Harriers. On 1 August 1973 the second DF/GA Hunter unit was formed at Wittering when 45 Squadron was split into

two to create 58 Squadron. Actually, the two units were 'squadrons' in name only, the Hunters being divided between the units, with 58 Squadron's allocation receiving the owl motif in place of 45 Squadron's famous 'Flying Camel', and the red diamonds of the flanking bar marking being repainted in green. A year later the fleet, which for engineering purposes at least was a single squadron with two flights, was pooled again under the title 'Hunter Wing'.

No. 229 OCU finally closed at Chivenor in September 1974. Thereafter, a dedicated training school – the Tactical Weapons Unit (TWU) at RAF Brawdy in Pembrokeshire – led to the slimming down and eventual disbandment of the Hunter force at Wittering. Nos 45 and 58 Squadrons were disbanded on 26 July 1976. At its peak TWU operated about seventy Hunters in four 'shadow squadrons' – nos 45, 63, 79 and 234 – which, in time of crisis, would have become first-line squadrons. In 1978 the TWU was split into two, Brawdy becoming a Hawk station (1 TWU), while all the Hunters moved to 2 TWU at Lossiemouth, Scotland. In 1980 2 TWU moved to Chivenor, where it too received the Hawks.

Overleaf: FGA.9 XG130 of 1 Squadron at West Raynham on 28 August 1968. This Kingston-built F.6 was first flown on 14 August 1956 by Duncan Simpson and subsequently served with 63 and 66 Squadrons before returning to Hawkers in 1959 for conversion to FGA.9 standard. XG130 served in 1 Squadron until August 1972 when it joined 45 Squadron then re-forming at West Raynham, Norfolk. On 17 June 1974 Flt Lt J.C. Firth (of 58 Squadron) abandoned XG130/'61' in cloud near Melton Mowbray and ejected safely. (*Adrian Balch*)

FGA.9 XG207 of 54 Squadron at RAF Valley on 10 August 1968. Built at Kingston as an F.6, XG207 was flown for the first time on 4 October 1956 by David Lockspeiser and was delivered to 19 MU on the 29th. XG207 served with 93 and 1 Squadrons before conversion to FGA.9 standard, being delivered in January 1960. (*Adrian Balch*)

Flt Lt Chris Humphrey of
1 Squadron landed with the nose
leg stuck in the 'up' position, at El
Adem, Libya, during APC
deployment from RAF West
Raynham on 6 April 1969. Chris was
tragically killed a few years later in a
Harrier flying accident in Germany.
(*Neal J. Wharton*)

F.6 XF382 of 229 OCU at RAF
Coningsby on 12 July 1972. This
aircraft was first issued to
65 Squadron and it went on to serve
with 92 Squadron and the Day
Fighters' Conversion Squadron
(DFCS) at West Raynham, being
converted to FGA.9 and transferring
to Brawdy in October 1976 where it
joined 79 'Shadow' Squadron.
(*Adrian Balch*)

FGA.9 XK137/D of 45 Squadron airborne from Wittering in December 1972. This Kingston-built F.6 was flown for the first time on 11 March 1957 by Duncan Simpson and was delivered to the RAF on 8 May 1957. It served with 20 Squadron before returning to Hawkers on 2 January 1961 for conversion to FGA.9. It served with 43 Squadron before joining the 'Flying Camels' in 1965. (via *Gp Capt Hastings*)

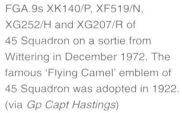

FGA.9s XK140/P, XF519/N, XG252/H and XG207/R of 45 Squadron on a sortie from Wittering in December 1972. The famous 'Flying Camel' emblem of 45 Squadron was adopted in 1922. (via *Gp Capt Hastings*)

Overleaf: GA.11 XE712 of FRADU at RNAS Yeovilton on 8 July 1972. This Blackpool-built F.4 was delivered to the RAF on 2 September 1959 and issued to 222 Squadron. It went on to serve with 43 Squadron and was converted to GA.11 standard, being delivered on 6 April 1962. In 1968 it joined 738 Squadron and subsequently joined the Yeovilton Station Flight. (*Adrian Balch*)

FGA.9 XG291/K of 45 Squadron in flight in December 1972. (via *Gp Capt Hastings*)

FGA.9s of 45 Squadron returning to Wittering in vic formation at sunset. (via *Gp Capt Hastings*)

Hunter 'Break!' (via *Gp Capt Hastings*)

Overleaf, above: Hunters of 229 OCU at RAF Chivenor on 23 August 1969. FGA.9 XG260/T, the nearest aircraft, was built as an F.6 at Kingston and first flown on 26 October 1956 by Duncan Simpson before being issued to 54 Squadron and converted to FGA.9 standard in 1960. Nine years later, on 13 September 1969, Hawkers bought the aircraft and converted it to FGA.74 (501). It was delivered to the Singaporean Air Force on 12 November 1970. (*Adrian Balch*)

Overleaf, below: FGA.9 XG207 of 79 'Shadow' Squadron/229 OCU, at Gibraltar on 21 September 1969. XG207 transferred to 45 Squadron on 15 October 1972, moving to 58 Squadron on 1 August 1973, and finally, to 2 TWU in 1980. (*Adrian Balch*)

Sqn Ldr Callum Kerr in FGA.9 XG261/'64' ripples off a SNEB pod at the Theddlethorpe Range in June 1974. Sqn Ldr Kerr was on the strength of 58 Squadron, but XG261 nominally belonged to the 'Flying Camels' squadron. XG261, which prior to joining 45 Squadron had served with 54 and 43 Squadrons, went to the TWU at Brawdy on 29 June 1976 when the 'Flying Camels' disbanded. (*MoD*)

FGA.9 XG228/'56' of 2 TWU/79 'Shadow' Squadron from RAF Brawdy, flown by the CO, Sqn Ldr Kenneth Becker, on 26 July 1984. This was its last flight before it was scrapped at RAF St Athan. (*BAe*)

Hunters of 237 OCU at RAF Lyneham on 2 August 1991. They were the last Hunters in RAF service. No. 237 OCU had been established in 1971 for RAF pilots who were to convert to the Blackburn Buccaneer S.2, the two-seat Hunters providing an Integrated Flight Instrumentation System (IFIS) as a link between the Hawk advanced trainer and the operational Buccaneers at RAF Honington. (*Adrian Balch*)

The last Hunters in RAF service were the ex-RAF and FAA two-seaters of 237 OCU at Honington, Suffolk. This organization had been established in 1971 to provide dual-control facilities for RAF pilots who were to convert to the HS Buccaneer S.2, sixty-two of which had been transferred from the FAA to the RAF, where they equipped 12 and 15 Squadrons at Honington. The two-seat Hunters provided an Integrated Flight Instrumentation System (IFIS) as a link between the Hawk advanced trainer and the operational Buccaneers at RAF Honington. No. 237 OCU later moved to Lossiemouth and was eventually disbanded in 1991. In all, some 1,972 Hunter aircraft flew in forty RAF (and five Royal Navy) squadrons, as well as in twenty-one overseas air forces. T.7 XL612 was the last Hunter in the UK to operate in a military capacity, being routinely used on intentional spinning exercises until it was finally retired by the Empire Test Pilots School (ETPS) in July 2001, fifty years to the month after WB188 first flew from Boscombe Down. The Hunter legend lives on, however, with some 114 potentially airworthy airframes located in fourteen countries around the world.

T.8C XF995 and T.7As XL616/D, XL568/C and WV318/A of No. 208 Squadron near Lossiemouth, 21 September 1993. Currently, WV318 (G-FFOX) is Delta Jets flagship at Kemble (where XF995 is also based), while XL616 (SE-DXH) flies from Brommen, Sweden, and XL568 is destined to become a static display in a museum. (*Adrian Balch*)

T.7 XL564 of the ETPS in the red, white and blue 'raspberry-ripple' scheme at Boscombe Down. This two-seater, and XL612, were the last of the school's fixed-wing fleet and were believed to be the only two swept-wing aircraft in the world that were routinely used on intentional spinning exercises. XL612, based at Boscombe since 7 May 1975, was the last Hunter in the UK to operate in a military capacity, flying for the last time on 10 August 2001, fifty years after WB188 first flew from Boscombe Down. (*Pat Barker*)

'You are old Hawker Hunter,'
The young man said,
'And your paintwork is no longer bright,
Yet I see that you constantly stagger aloft,
Do you think at your age that it's right?'

'Yes I'm old,' smiled the Hunter,
'As you observe,
Yet you're missing the pertinent thought,
Were it not for its age no antique would deserve
All the money for which it is bought.'

'But you're old AND outdated,'

The young man frowned,
'And your instruments ancient and plain.
Tell me, how can you navigate so close to the ground
Without using a digital brain?'

'In my youth,' yawned the Hunter,
'Pilots could fly
Using stopwatch and compass and map.
And I'm teaching them still to be Kings of the Sky,
Now be off . . . while I'm taking a nap.'
                    Anonymous, Wittering Review, *July 1976*

Index

74 ('Tiger') Squadron 32–7, 40, 51, 53–4, 58
92 (East India) Squadron 40–1, 70, 71–86
111 ('Treble One') Squadron 59–70, 71, 77, 80, 84

Acklington 40, 58
Aden 30, 43, 87, 91, 93, 95, 102, 103, 110, 117
Air Fighting Development Squadron (AFDS) 87
air speed records 9–10, 59
Aird, Flg Off George P. 59, 62
Airwork Services Ltd 131
Aked, Flg Off Alastair 43
Akrotiri, Cyprus 43, 52
Albrecht, Capt Pete (USAF) 127
Aldridge, Flt Lt Tony M. 63, 65, 70, 71, 72, 80, 86
Allchin, Flg Off Brian C. 71
Allied Command Europe Mobile Forces 124
Amman 52
Anwar, Flt Lt Hamid 71, 72
Armstrong Whitworth Aircraft Ltd 2, 8, 20, 32
Athens 80
Avions Fairey company 51
Aylett, Flt Lt George 71

Bacon, Sqn Ldr (now Air Cdre) G. 'Max' 112–13, 116–17, 120
Badger aircraft 113
Baginton see Coventry
Bahrain 92, 93, 95, 110
Bangkok 71, 116
Barcelona 68
Barnes, Lt Col William F. 9
Battle of Britain 71
Battle of Britain Day 86
Beagle aircraft 53
Bear aircraft 51
Beck, Flt Sgt Bill 59
Becker, Ken (pilot) 127
Bedford, Alfred William 'Bill' (pilot) 6, 10, 38
Beirut 52
Belgium 51
Bennett, Arthur 53–4

Beverley aircraft 43
Biggin Hill 16, 32
Bildeston 67
Bird-Wilson, Wg Cdr 11
Bison aircraft 51
Biss, Flt Lt Chan 71
Black Arrows display team 58, 59–70
Black Knights display team 13–18
Blackpool, Hawker production at 20, 27, 51, 60
Blue Diamonds display team 58, 70, 71–86
Blue Herons display team 131
Borneo 110, 113, 115, 117, 120
Boscombe Down 2, 3, 21, 148
Bragg, Flt Lt Bob 15, 17–18
Brawdy 26, 125, 131, 137
Britannia aircraft 93
Britannia Challenge Trophy 70
Broadhurst, ACM Sir Harry 60
Brown, Flt Lt Robin A. 28, 49
Brüggen Wing (2nd TAF) 27, 30, 32, 48, 49
Brunei 110
Brussels Air Show 7
Buccaneer aircraft 125, 131,148
Bullard, Flt Sgt Ken 30
Bullen, Frank (pilot) 6
Burns, Flt Lt Bobby 21

Cadwallader, Flg Off Ian 32, 36
Calvey, Flt Lt 11
Cameron, Flg Off Crawford 71
Camm 1, 2
Campbell, Donald 58
Canberra aircraft 3, 11, 112–13, 115, 117, 124, 131
Carpenter, Flt Lt Ray 'Chips' 71
Carr, Sqn Ldr Peter 51, 54, 58
Champniss, Sqn Ldr Phil 102–3, 110
Charlton, Dennis 4
Chase, Bob (aviator) 28
Chase, Mick 63, 80
Cheshire, AVM Walter 40
Chilbolton 2
Chivenor 13, 22, 23, 27, 32, 37, 125, 126, 127–8, 137
Church Fenton 40
Churchill, Winston 1

Clavering, Flg Off Douglas 116
Coltishall 34, 36, 54, 67, 87, 126, 127–8
Comet I airliner 59
Cossey, Bob 51
Coventry (Baginton), Armstrong Whitworth at 2, 8, 20, 32
Crisham, AVM W.J. 'Paddy' 41
Crusader aircraft 43
Curtis, Sqn Ldr Chris 51, 53
Curtis, Plt Off K.R. 'Curt' 14–18
Cyprus 32, 41, 43, 50, 52–3, 58, 71, 74, 80, 84

Davies, Flt Lt Tony 34
Davis, John (aviator) 52
Day Fighter Leaders' School (DFLS) 18, 51
Deacon, SAC Ray 93, 103, 107
Dean, Tony (aviator) 33, 36
de Haviland company 1, 7, 62
Denmark 40–1, 51
Dennis, Wg Cdr D.F. 21
Derry, John (pilot) 6, 7
Dimmock, Lt 65
Dixon, Sqn Ldr Bob 41
Dodd, Flt Lt Basil 21–2
Duke, Sqn Ldr Neville 3, 6, 7, 9–10, 30, 38
Dunsfold, Surrey 7, 9
Duxford 40, 58

Eastleigh 92
Egypt 32, 43, 53, 95
Empire Test Pilots School (ETPS) 20, 21, 22, 148
English Electric 3, 38, 86
Exercise Vigilant 34, 36

Faisal II, King 43
Farnborough Air Show 3, 6, 7, 62, 63, 65, 67, 68, 71, 86
Farnborough Royal Aircraft Establishment 15–16, 20, 21
Fassberg Wing (2nd TAF) 27
Fighter Weapons School, Leconfield 20
Fighting Cocks display team 13
Firebirds display team 86
Fleet Air Arm see Royal Navy
Fleet Requirements and Air Direction Unit

(FRADU) 131
Fokker company 51
Folland company 87
Fort Harib, Yemen 102–3, 107
Franco, General 125
Fraser, Hugh 110
Freeman, Flt Lt Taff 71
Frick, Flt Lt Heinz 116, 117
Funnell, Tony (aviator) 28

Garratt, Flg Off Dave 59, 60
Geilenkirchen Wing (2nd TAF) 27, 30, 48, 49
German jet designs 1, 2
Germany 23, 27, 30, 32, 48, 50
Gibraltar 125
Gill, Flt Lt Derek G. 71
Gloster 1
Gnat aircraft 87, 90
Goodwin, Flg Off Dave 59
Grimer, David (aviator) 77
Grimshaw, Flt Lt Frank 71
Gütersloh 32, 50

Habbaniyah 43
Haggerty, Mike (pilot) 28
Hal Far, Malta 41
Hall, Flt Lt 'Straw' 60
Hamilton, Flg Off P.V.L. 'Pete' 14
Hardacre, John (instructor) 22
Harrier aircraft 32, 51, 131, 137
Hawk aircraft 137
Hawker company 1–3, 7–8, 37–8, 51 see also Hunter aircraft
Hawker Siddeley company 90
Hayward, Eric 7, 8, 9, 10, 60, 90
Hazell, LAC Ken 34, 36
Heather-Hayes, Dai 111
Henderson, George 95
Higgs, Flg Off Ron 41
Highton, Flt Lt Pete 86
Hilton, Flg Off Tony 34
Hobson, Sqn Ldr (later Wg Cdr) Mike 40–1, 62, 67, 126
Hobson, Wg Cdr Rick 126
Holland 51
Homes, Sqn Ldr C.J. 49
Hong Kong 112
Honington 148

Horsham St Faith 32–7 *passim*, 40, 51, 90
Horton, Flg Off Barry 127
Howe, Sqn Ldr (later AVM) 58
Humphreyson, Flt Lt 102
Hunter aircraft
    designed by Camm 1
    prototypes 2–3, 6, 7–8
    gun-pack change 4
    first production models 9
    breaks world speed record 9–10
    enters RAF service 11, 13–14
    charisma 12
    early accidents 14–20
    trainer aircraft 20, 23, 26
    spinning trials 21–2
    with 2nd TAF in Germany 27–32, 48,
        50
    with 'Tiger' Squadron 32–4, 51
    F.6 developed 37–8, 40
    in Cyprus 40–1, 43
    overseas orders 51
    in Middle East 52–4
    supersonic 54, 58
    F.6 phased out 86
    ground-attack aircraft (FGA.9s) 51,
        87–31 *passim*
    FGA.9s withdrawn 131, 137
    last of the Hunters 148
Hunter Strike Wing 93, 107
Hunting-Percival company 87
Hymans, Plt Off (later Flt Lt) Roger E.
    50, 69

Immig, Capt Richard G. 13–18
India 51
Indian Air Force 87, 126
Indonesia 110, 112–13, 115–17, 120
Iran, Shah of 80
Iraq 43, 92, 93
Israel 52
Ives, Sqn Ldr W. 19–20

Jaguar aircraft 131, 137
Jarvis, Sqn Ldr John 16, 17
Javelin aircraft 2, 34, 36, 113, 116, 117
Jennings, Wg Cdr John 102, 103, 107
Jet Provost aircraft 86, 87, 90
Jever Wing (2nd TAF) 27, 30, 40, 48, 50
Johnson, Flt Lt Martin 102, 107
Jones, David 37
Jones, Sqn Ldr G. 'Spike' 125, 127, 131
Jordan 52

Kassim, General Abdul Karim 92
Kelly, Ned (pilot) 43
Kent, Johnny (Station Commander) 17
Kenya 92, 95
Kestrel aircraft 51
Khormaksar, Aden 87, 91, 92, 93, 95,
    107
Khrushchev, Nikita 50, 53
Kingsley, Terry 52
Kingston-upon-Thames, Hawker
    production at 2, 7, 8, 20, 23, 27
Kuwait 92, 93, 126

Lampard, Chris 111
Land Speed Record 58
Langley, Bucks. 7
Larnaca 53
Latham, Sqn Ldr (later AVM) Peter A.
    67, 68, 69
Le Bourget 60
Lebanon 52, 53
Leconfield 20, 58, 71, 72, 86
Leuchars 13, 32, 40
Libya 10, 53
Lightning aircraft 37, 38, 54, 58, 84, 86,
    117, 126, 127–8, 131, 137
Linton-on-Ouse 32, 43
Lossiemouth 23, 26, 131, 137, 148

McPherson, Flt Lt J. 19
Malaysia 110, 112, 113, 115, 116, 117
Malta 41
Manby Flying College 27, 126
Marham 18, 19
Martin, Jack (USAF) 51
Martin, Flt Lt Peter 116
Mason, Francis K. 12
Mercer, Flt Lt (later Sqn Ldr) Brian 67,
    68, 71, 79, 80, 84, 86
Merriman, Alan (pilot) 22
Meteor aircraft 15, 17–18, 27, 30, 32, 34,
    59, 126
Middle East 51, 87, 92, 93
Middle East Air Force (MEAF) 50
Middleton St George 32, 40, 41, 62, 71,
    86
MiG aircraft 102, 113, 117
Ministry of Defence (MoD) 90
Ministry of Supply (MoS) 2, 51
Mitchell aircraft 112, 116, 117
Muharraq, Bahrain 93, 110, 111
Murphy, Frank (pilot) 6, 9, 27
Mustang aircraft 112, 113, 117

Nairobi 92, 95
Nasser, President Abdul 53, 95
NATO 40, 117, 124, 127
    AIRCENT gun-firing competition 83
Nicosia 41, 50, 52
Noble, Flt Lt Bernard 'Nobby' 14–18, 21
Norman, Flt Lt M.J. 19–20
North Weald 27, 40, 59, 60

Oakden, Flt Lt Don 71
Odiham 13, 14–18, 40, 62, 63, 67
Oldenburg Wing (2nd TAF) 27, 30, 48,
    50
Operation Musketeer 32
Operational Conversion Units (OCUs) 13
    see also Chivenor; Pembrey

Pakistan 51
Pakistan Air Force 71, 72
Paris Aeronautical Salon display 60, 68
Patch, AVM H.L. 18
Pembrey 13, 20
Pendrey, Bill (radar controller) 16, 17, 18

Perry, Pete (aviator) 28
Peru 51
Phantom aircraft 32, 59, 131, 137
Pike, ACM Sir Thomas 59–60, 62
Pioneer CCI aircraft 120
Pollock, Flt Lt Alan 125, 127, 128, 131
Pountain, Wg Cdr Stuart G. 19
Powers, Gary (USAF) 50

Radfan, Yemen 95, 103, 110, 117
Rao, Flt Lt 126
Ray, Philip 84
Red Arrows display team 86
Red Pelicans display team 86
Redhouse, Flg Off Colin J. 'Chunky' 14
Rhodesians 126
Richards, Tony (observer) 6, 7
Richardson, Ken (flight commander) 40
Rix, Richard D. (armourer) 91
Roberts, Flt Lt Robbie 71
Robinson, Flg Off (later AVM) Boz 33,
    34, 36, 37
Rowe, Snr Artificer Jack 26
Royal Aero Club 70
Royal Air Force (RAF) 127, 148
    Air Support Command 127
    Fighter Command 59, 70
    Strike Command 127
    Transport Command 124
    see also Tactical Air Force (TAF), 2nd
Royal Australian Air Force (RAAF) 116
Royal Navy 1–2, 23, 26, 43, 125, 131,
    148
Royal New Zealand Air Force (RNZAF)
    32
Russian aircraft 51, 52–3, 112
Rustington 10

Sabre aircraft 9, 11, 19, 27, 28, 30, 48,
    86, 116
Saddam Hussein 43
St Clair, Flt Lt Brian E. 71
Sandys, Duncan 48, 51
Sarawak 110, 113, 115, 116
Sea Fury aircraft 7
Sea Harrier aircraft 26
Sea Hawk aircraft 2, 7, 43, 65
Seaton, Sqn Ldr 11
Second World War 1, 48, 71
Severne, John (CO) 28
Shackleton aircraft 93, 95, 110, 120
Simpson, Duncan (pilot) 11
Singapore 51, 110, 116, 120
Skrydstrup 40–1
Slinfold, Sussex 16
Smith, Flt Lt Dick 117
South East Asia Treaty Organisation
    (SEATO) 110
Soviet Union 1 *see also* Russian aircraft
Spitfire aircraft 71
Stint, Cpl Dave 32
Stoker, Flt Lt Bill 71, 72
Stoker, Mr William 72
Storey, Group Captain 'Twinkle' 111
Stradishall 32, 40, 120, 124

Strong, Flt Lt Chris 71
Strong, Sqn Ldr C.J. 124
Suez Canal 32
Sukano, President 117
Supermarine company 1, 2
    Attacker aircraft 2
    Swift aircraft 2, 10, 11, 12, 30, 32
Sweden 51
Switzerland 11, 51
Swoffer, Flg Off P.A. 'Pat' 14–18
Sycamore aircraft 41
Syria 43, 52

Tactical Air Force (TAF), 2nd 23, 27, 28,
    30, 32, 48, 49, 50
Tactical Air Navigation (TACAN) system
    26
Tactical Weapons Unit (TWU) 137
Tangmere 16–17, 32, 50
Tappenden, Sgt Roy 59
Taylor, Flt Lt Pete 71
Tehran 80
Tengah, Singapore 110, 116, 117, 124
Thornaby 41
Thurley, Flg Off Michael 60
Topp, Sqn Ldr (later Air Cdre) Roger L.
    59–60, 62–4, 67
Torrey Canyon 125
Tower Bridge, flight under 128, 131
Trevaskis, Sir Kennedy 95
Tumility, Sqn Ldr Richard 18–19
Twell, R. 18
Typhoon aircraft 1

United Kingdom 1
United States of America 1, 43, 52

Valley 127–8
Vampire aircraft 14, 16, 18, 28
Venom aircraft 11, 27, 43, 48, 71, 87,
    112, 117
Vickery, Flt Lt John 81
Volkers, Flg Off E.J. 'John' 91

Wade, Sqn Ldr T.S. 'Wimpy' 3, 6
Walton, Flt Lt B.K. 'Wally' 125, 127
Waterbeach 32, 40, 124–5
Watford, Flt Lt B. 19
Wattisham 13, 32, 50, 58, 62, 63, 67,
    127–8
Westland Whirlwind helicopters 8, 116
West Raynham 7, 11, 13, 18, 27, 36, 54,
    90, 125, 127–8, 131, 137
Wildenrath Wing (2nd TAF) 27
Wilkinson, Geoff (pilot) 28
Williams, Flt Lt G. 102
Williams, Lt Cdr Neville, RN 18–19
Wittering 131, 137
World Absolute Air Speed Record 9–10
Wyk, Flt Lt Piet van 85–6

Yeardley, Dennis (instructor) 22
Yellowjacks display team 86
Yemen 95, 102–3, 107, 124
Yeovilton 131